Englisch lernen mit Berlitz®

Maeve Binchy

Travelling Hopefully

D1983789

Berlitz Publishing
München • New York • Singapur

Berlitz Englisch lernen mit Maeve Binchy
Travelling Hopefully

Vokabelerklärungen und Übungen: Christina Sanchez
Layout: Ute Weber
Cover-Gestaltung: Dominik Lommer
Projektleitung: Eva Betz

Berlitz Publishing
Mies-van-der-Rohe-Straße 1
D-80807 München

Satz: Franzis print & media GmbH, München
Druck: CS Druck Cornelsen Stürtz, Berlin
Printed in Germany
ISBN 978-3-468-79237-3

1. 2. 3. 4. 5. 12 11 10 09 08

Inhalt

Liebe Leserin, lieber Leser,

mit den herzerfrischenden Kurzgeschichten von Maeve Binchy halten Sie endlich ein Englischbuch in der Hand, das Sie garantiert nicht mehr weglegen wollen. Und vor lauter Romantik und Spannung merken Sie vielleicht gar nicht, dass Sie ganz nebenbei auch Ihre Englischkenntnisse gehörig auffrischen und erweitern. Damit Ihr Lesevergnügen nicht durch das Nachschlagen unbekannter Wörter gemindert wird, sind die schwierigsten Vokabeln im Text blau markiert und in der Marginalspalte übersetzt. Interessante Wörter, die in einer Infobox erklärt werden, sind zusätzlich mit einem Sternchen gekennzeichnet. Alle übersetzten Wörter sind außerdem im Wörterverzeichnis im Anhang zusammengefasst.
Allein beim Schmökern in den Kurzgeschichten können Sie sehr viel dazulernen. Vielleicht möchten Sie aber auch Ihr Grammatikwissen und Ihre Vokabelkenntnisse zusätzlich erweitern oder aber Ihr Textverständnis prüfen. Zu diesem Zweck finden Sie auf jeder Doppelseite knifflige und unterhaltsame Übungen. Die Vokabeln aus dem Text werden dort noch einmal verwendet und bleiben dadurch viel besser im Gedächtnis haften – so können Sie später leichter darauf zurückgreifen. Selbstverständlich sind auch die Lösungen zu allen Übungen im Anhang abgedruckt.

Und nun wünschen wir Ihnen viel Spaß beim Lesen!
Ihre Berlitz-Redaktion

Miss Vogel's Vacation

Urlaub

Miss Vogel was surprised that she had never married. Not so much upset as surprised. When she was young everyone thought Victoria Vogel would surely be one of the first in the neighborhood to walk down an aisle. Fair-haired, soft and pretty, a great homemaker, she even made dresses for herself and her sisters and their friends, as well as baking delicious desserts for any event where good cooking was needed.

zum Traualtar schreiten • blond • Hausfrau

The young Miss Vogel had an agreeable manner with everyone; no future mother-in-law would stand in her way, no family would object to the girl who worked pleasantly in her father's bakery. She was much in demand to dance at the weddings of her many friends, and although she caught the bride's bouquet on many occasions, it never led to a wedding of her own.

freundlich

begehrt

Strauß

Miss Vogel didn't look back on her girlhood in New York as a lonely time; she hadn't yearned always for a beau of her own. She always thought there was one around the next corner. She lived happily over the bakery and didn't really notice the years go by.

gesehnt • Schatz

bemerkte

There were so many other things to think about. Like her mother's illness. The others were all married by the time Miss Vogel's mother took to her bed, so she did the nursing, which made sense because she lived at home.

bettlägerig wurde • Pflege

And when her mother died and her father became gloomy and lost interest in his work, she had to work all that much harder in the bakery to keep it going. There was a manager, of course, Tony Bari. They spent long hours together trying to see how the bills could

trübsinnig • am Laufen zu halten

be paid, the overheads reduced, and the whole enterprise made sound.
Everyone thought one day they might marry.
Miss Vogel didn't really think they would, even though she would have been happy had their quick embraces led to a proposal.
But she was a practical woman and realized that Tony Bari was very interested in money and had told her several times that any sensible man in business was looking for a rich wife. Miss Vogel knew she wasn't in this category, and even though she did like his company, his big broad smile and the way his mustache tickled her cheek, she didn't weep when he told her he had finally met a lady of property and invited her to his wedding.
Not long after, Miss Vogel's father went to the hospital, and it was known that he would not come out. Tony Bari bought the business. His new wife did not think it appropriate that Miss Vogel continue to work and live there, so, at the age of thirty, she was unemployed.
People said Tony Bari had not paid enough, and indeed, after it had been divided between her sisters and brothers there was very little left.

Unkosten • Unternehmen • saniert
Umarmungen
Schnurrbart • kitzelte • Wange • weinte • wohlhabend
angemessen
tatsächlich

Übung 1 Ergänzen Sie die fehlenden Buchstaben der englischen Begriffe.

1. A woman whose husband has died is called a w _ _ _ _.
2. The opposite of male is _ _ _ _ _ _.
3. Janet was unhappy with her life.
   She was _ _ s _ _ n _ _ _ t _ _ with it.
4. Most people laugh when you _ _ c _ _ _ them.
5. Tony Bari did not have a beard. He had a _ u _ _ _ c _ _.
6. When someone _ e _ _ s, he or she is usually sad.
7. In the end, Tony did not marry Miss Vogel but a lady of
   p _ _ _ _ _ ty.

Miss Vogel had nowhere to live, she had no real qualifications to get a good job anywhere, but with her customary good humor she decided to wait until something turned up. Then she saw a position as a type of janitor or superintendent in a small, new apartment building. A lot of the residents were female, and they had specifically sought a woman super. Miss Vogel, with her calm, pleasant manner, seemed ideal, and she now had a two-room apartment, with an address in a fine part of town.

Her friends were pleased for her.

'You'll meet very classy folk now,' they said.

Miss Vogel didn't mind whether they were classy or not, just as long as they were nice. And mainly they were.

She became involved in all their lives. She walked the little yapping dog, unsuitably called Beauty, for Janet, the discontented widow in Number One.

She baby-sat for the teenage daughter of Heather, who was a workaholic advertising supreme in Number Two.

She took in the flowers and arranged them for Number Three, where Francesca the attractive mistress of two businessmen lived. Tactfully, Miss Vogel made sure these two gentlemen never coincided on a visit.

ihr eigen

Hausmeister • Hausverwalter • Bewohner • weiblich • ausdrücklich • gesucht • Hausverwalterin • feine Leute

die meisten • beteiligt • kläffend • unglücklich • Witwe • Führungskraft

Liebhaberin • sich … zufällig trafen

info

Wenn Sie in einem Text einem unbekannten englischen Wort begegnen, können Sie unterschiedliche Strategien anwenden, um dessen Bedeutung zu erschließen.
In manchen Fällen kennen Sie vielleicht ein ganz ähnlich aussehendes Wort. Das kann ein deutsches Wort oder ein Fremdwort sein, vielleicht aber auch eine französische, lateinische, spanische oder italienische Vokabel, die Sie noch aus der Schule kennen.
So könnten Sie sich z. B. mustache über das französische moustache herleiten oder specific über das deutsche Wort spezifisch.

She spent a lot of time in Number Four, where Marion sat and looked out the window, sad because her husband came home so rarely.

There were many others in the building whose lives were familiar to Miss Vogel. Her sisters sometimes said these must be rich, spoiled people who lacked nothing in their lives, but Miss Vogel didn't agree. As she sat in beautifully decorated apartments and drank coffee from a fine china cup or soda from cut-crystal glassware, Miss Vogel knew that unease and unhappiness didn't fly out the window just because you had money. A lot of the people had even more worries than the Vogel family ever had. Sometimes she went past the old bakery where Tony Bari had built a big business with his wife's money. It was now a delicacies shop, and people faxed in their orders for sandwiches, which were delivered to their offices. Imagine!

There were three children. Miss Vogel watched them grow up. She would have liked to have met them properly and known them, to have been invited into the store where she, too, had lived as a child.

But Tony Bari's wife never seemed to want her around.

bekannt • denen nichts fehlte

Porzellan • Limo • Kummer

geliefert

aufwachsen

info

West Coast: Die Staaten an der Westküste der USA. Unter diesen ist Kalifornien ein besonders beliebtes Reiseziel.

Disneyland: Disneyland ist ein berühmter Freizeitpark in Anaheim, Kalifornien. Neben den üblichen Fahrgeschäften begegnen dem Besucher dort auch lebensgroße Figuren aus den Walt-Disney-Filmen.

Universal Studios: Im Freizeitpark der Universal Studios in Hollywood dreht sich alles ums Thema Film. Man kann dort auch Original-Filmsets besichtigen.

Miss Vogel thought this was sad. She had always been welcoming and kind to the woman who had come to live there only because of her father's dollars. But then, you couldn't make people like you if they didn't.

Her days and nights were never empty or lonely, because of all the people in the apartments. Miss Vogel did not have what anyone would call a great life of her own, but she went through all theirs, their hopes and dreams for Thanksgiving and Christmas, who would come home, where they would be invited, what they would cook. Their diets for the new year, how many days a week working out at the gym, low-fat foods to be stocked in the freezer. Then she went through their new wardrobes for spring. None seemed to notice Miss Vogel didn't buy spring clothes, plan to lose ten pounds every January, or discuss where she went for Thanksgiving or Christmas.

She was a listening person, not a talking person.

She was interested in their lives.

Now it was time to talk about vacations.

Janet was going to Arizona with her sister, so naturally there was the matter of Beauty, the bad-tempered little dog, Beauty didn't like kennels, so perhaps Miss Vogel …

Heather could take only a week and not one day more away from works, so she would fly to Los Angeles. This way, she could fit in one or two meetings on the West Coast* as well as take fourteen-year-old Heidi to Disneyland* and Universal Studios*, so it would be a fantastic holiday for the child. But there was simply no time to get her any vacation clothes. Could Miss Vogel manage … one Saturday morning possibly? Just a quick trip to the department store?

Francesca was going to spend one week with one man and the other with the second man, but she had told each she was going to a health spa for the week she would not be with him. Would Miss Vogel mind very

Thanksgiving: Erntedank
working out: trainieren •
gym: Fitnessstudio •
stocked: gelagert •
wardrobes: Garderoben •
spring: Frühling
bad-tempered: übellaunig •
kennels: Hundepension
fit in: dazwischennehmen
department store: Kaufhaus
health spa: Kur

much taking the bus to this town two miles away, where the spa actually was, and mailing two postcards for her? You see, men were so possessive and so suspicious these days, and one didn't want to do anything silly.

aufzugeben • besitzergreifend • argwöhnisch • eine Dummheit • fröhlich • Gasthof

Marion in Number Four was uncharacteristically cheerful because she and her husband were going to a quiet inn – he said he would like time to talk properly. That had to be good, Marion said, vacations were a time when people found new relationships if they had none or cemented an existing one that needed to be patched up.

festigten • gekittet

That was the wonderful thing about vacations, wasn't it, Marion had said over and over.

Miss Vogel didn't know. She had never had a vacation. There had never been the opportunity, the money, or the time. And now, at fifty-three, there seemed little point in hoping she would find a new relationship, and there wasn't an old one to cement.

Beziehung

Tony Bari and his wife and children were going to Italy. Her sisters, brothers, and their families were going to a lake where they rented chalets every year. Nice for the cousins to get to know each other and keep in touch, they said.

Ferienhäuser • in Kontakt zu bleiben

Übung 2 Welche der angegebenen Möglichkeiten ist die richtige? Kreuzen Sie sie bitte an.

1. Francesca asked Miss Vogel to mail a postcard from
- ☐ Disneyland.
- ☐ Rome.
- ☐ a health spa.

2. Marion was usually not very cheerful because
- ☐ she was very ill.
- ☐ she had problems with her husband.
- ☐ she did not like the other residents.

None of them ever thought it might be nice for Miss Vogel to get to know them all and keep in touch, too. But then, she would be out of place. An elderly aunt on her own.
All the holidays seemed to come together. Miss Vogel would have a very empty building to look after. But she enthused about their trips, as she had enthused for so many years about everything they did.
She did all she was asked to do. She studied the feeding schedules of the small, aggressive Beauty to reassure Janet. She took Heidi on an outing to Bloomingdale's and with Heather's dollars bought her bright-colored clothes to wear in the California sun. She planned the two bus trips so she could send the deceiving postcards for Francesca. She helped Marion pack romantic negligees for her week in the country inn.
And, of course, she would do all the other things that made them think Miss Vogel was an angel. She would turn out their lights, pull their drapes at different times each evening, sort their mail, so, when they came back, it would be in a neat pile on their hall table. She would see their garments were returned from the dry cleaner and hung in their closets; she would admit

fehl am Platz • älter

sich um … kümmern • begeisterte sich

Zeitpläne • beruhigen • Ausflug • (ein Kaufhaus in New York) • trügerisch

Engel • Vorhänge • Stapel • Diele • dafür sorgen • Kleidung • Reinigung • Schränke

3. Miss Vogel did not go to the lake with her brothers and sisters and their families because
- ☐ they never asked her to come with them.
- ☐ she thought that it was too hot there.
- ☐ she was afraid of travelling by plane.

4. When Miss Vogel went to Bloomingdale's with Heidi, they bought
- ☐ negligees.
- ☐ drapes.
- ☐ clothes for the summer holidays.

Innenausstatter • Erzählungen

a television repairman here and an interior decorator there and listen to their holiday tales and look at their holiday photos with great interest on their return.

Hektik • tatsächlich • herbeigewinkt

Often there was fuss and near hysteria at the actual time of departure; limousines had not been ordered in advance, for example, or taxis could not be hailed on the New York streets.

vorbeugen • geheim • Abholort

This year, Miss Vogel decided to cut through all the drama and found a neighborhood car service. She spoke to Frank, a man with a tired, kind face, who was at the desk, telling him she had four trips over two days, to La Guardia Airport for Heather and Heidi, to Grand Central for Janet, to Penn Station for Marion and her husband, and some secret pickup place in New Jersey for Francesca.

Provision • müde

'What commission are you looking for?' Frank asked wearily.

Tarif

'Oh no,' Miss Vogel said. 'I was only trying to arrange something for the people in my building. They'll all pay you the rate. I don't want anything … I don't want anything for myself.'

'You must be the only person in the world who doesn't, then,' said Frank.

'It's just their vacations. They get very fussed, you know the way people do?'

'I don't know the way people do,' Frank said. 'I've never had a vacation.'

Miss Vogel gave him a big smile. 'Do you know neither have I? We must be the only people in the world who haven't.'

das Eis zwischen ihnen war gebrochen • ermittelten

A bond was established between them, and they worked out the times he would be there to pick up the holiday-makers.

höflich • pünktlich

He was courteous and punctual, but more than that he was kind. He waited while Janet kissed Beauty goodbye; he told Heidi she'd love Disneyland – everyone came back from it a new person; he explained to Francesca that he was a genius at finding out-of-the-way spots in New Jersey; he told Marion and her husband that an inn in the countryside was the very best vacation anyone could choose.

Miss Vogel was sorry when the last had gone. She enjoyed Frank's company. She would miss regular visits when she always found time to make him a coffee and give him some of her own home-baked shortbread.

To her surprise, he turned up again.

'I was wondering, Miss Vogel, if you and I should have a vacation in New York,' he began tentatively. 'We could pretend we were tourists here and see it through their eyes.' He looked at her, hoping that she would not laugh at this or dismiss it as a ridiculous idea.

'A vacation in New York City?' she said thoughtfully.

'Well, a lot of people do, you know.' Frank was defensive. 'I drive them to places. I should know.'

'That will be great,' said Miss Vogel. 'But first I have to do a bit of fussing. That's essential.'

'Yes, I'll come around tomorrow morning. Does that give you time enough to fuss?' he asked.

Miss Vogel worked out that she could take a five-hour vacation each day. Then she ironed her clothes care-

Meister • abgelegene Orte • Land • regelmäßig • Buttergebäck • tauchte … auf • zögernd • so tun als ob • abtun • lächerlich • unbedingt erforderlich

Übung 3

Bringen Sie die Buchstaben der Wörter in Klammern in die richtige Reihenfolge und vervollständigen Sie dann die folgenden Sätze.

1. Marion and her husband went to an inn in the ________________ (sriuytocdne).

2. Miss Vogel liked Frank because he was a very ________________ (eoturcosu) person.

3. Whenever Frank came to visit her, Miss Vogel gave him home-baked ____________________ (retbshroda).

legte sich ... zurecht • Schönheitssalon

fully and laid out a different outfit for each outing. She went to a beauty parlor on the corner and got her hair and her nails done.

Absätze • Wettervorhersage

She prepared several picnic lunches they could have and left them ready in the freezer. She got new heels on her comfortable shoes. She checked the weather forecast. She was ready for her vacation.

They went to Ellis Island* and spent the day looking at where their grandparents had come into the United States from Italy and Germany, Ireland and Sweden.

wette

'I bet they were four young people who never had time for a vacation once they got here,' Miss Vogel said.

abenteuerlustig

Nachkommen

'But they must have been adventurous young people,' Frank replied, 'not the kind of folk who would like to believe their descendants would be stay-at-homes.'

The next day they went to the World Trade Center* to see the view and then back uptown to the zoo. Afterward, they walked in Central Park* in the sunshine.

kameradschaftlich

They drove together companionably to the town where they had to mail Francesca's postcards and talked about how odd life was with so many people living a lie – Francesca herself and the two married men who were each

info

Die Insel Ellis Island im Hudson River vor New York war lange Zeit der Sitz der Einwanderungsbehörde und somit die erste Anlaufstelle für Einwanderer in die Vereinigten Staaten. Heute können die Abfertigungshallen dort besichtigt werden.

Das World Trade Center erlangte durch den Anschlag, welcher 2001 auf die Zwillingstürme verübt wurde, traurige Berühmtheit. Vor dem Einsturz beherbergten die Gebäude Büros und Geschäfte.

Der Central Park ist die grüne Lunge von New York. In diesem wunderschönen öffentlichen Naherholungsgebiet gehen die New Yorker joggen, fahren Rad oder machen einfach einen Spaziergang.

taking her off for a week. They went to Chinatown * and on a tour of the stock exchange on Wall Street*. They went back to where Miss Vogel grew up and looked at the big delicacies shop, so much changed in appearance since her youth. They went to see where Frank was raised, changed so very much from when he was a boy. He pointed out where he had lived with his wife for three years a long time ago, and also the hospital where she had died.

mit ihr fortfuhren • Börse

aufgewachsen war • zeigte ihr

Neither had ever been to Carnegie Hall*, so they booked a concert.

And as she had seen a ball game only on television, never in reality, they went to Yankee Stadium*.

And the week flew by.

Frank helped Miss Vogel to sort the mail, arrange the curtains, and arrange deliveries for the tenants. Miss Vogel went to the car-service office and brightened it up by washing the curtains and putting some colourful ornaments around.

The next week, they could no longer afford five hours a day for vacation. Like everyone else in New York, they would now know that feeling which said the holiday was over.

verging wie im Flug • Mieter • verschönerte

Verzierung • sich leisten

info

Chinatown ist ein Stadtviertel von New York, das überwiegend von Chinesen bewohnt wird. Auch die meisten Schilder sind in chinesischer Sprache geschrieben, sodass sich der Besucher nach Asien versetzt fühlt.

Die Wall Street ist das Zentrum des New Yorker Finanzdistrikts. In dieser Straße findet man neben diversen Banken auch die New Yorker Börse.

Die Carnegie Hall ist eine über hundert Jahre alte Konzerthalle, in welcher sowohl klassische als auch Popkonzerte stattfinden.

Im Yankee Stadium, einem Baseballstadion in der New Yorker Bronx, finden die Heimspiele der Mannschaft New York Yankees statt.

But for Frank and Miss Vogel, there was something new and wonderful. No longer did they keep their thoughts to themselves, there was someone with whom to talk over the events of the day. Not only holiday memories, but what was happening in the real world as well.

So when Frank drove Heather and Heidi back from the airport, he could report that mother and daughter were hardly speaking and that the girl had been left alone in her hotel room looking at television, since Heather was **tied up** in meetings all day.

Miss Vogel could tell him that something very **odd** had happened in Francesca's life – perhaps both men had **proposed marriage** to her, both would leave their wives, but she wanted neither. Francesca was lying down with a cold compress on her eyes, trying to get the **courage** to tell them.

Janet told Frank in the car her holiday with her sister had been a huge mistake – there would be no more family get-togethers. What did people want family for, anyway? A good dog was worth twenty sisters.

Marion told Miss Vogel that her **rat of** a husband had taken her to the inn only to tell her he was leaving her. And amazingly, Marion didn't really mind all that

tied up: beschäftigt • odd: seltsam • proposed marriage: einen Heiratsantrag gemacht • courage: Mut • rat of: Mistkerl von

Übung 4 In den Ferien ist viel passiert.
Sind die folgenden Aussagen wahr oder falsch?
Tragen Sie ein T für true oder ein F für false in die Kästchen ein.

1. ☐ Heather and Heidi had spent lots of time together.
2. ☐ Francesca had told her two lovers that she didn't want to marry either of them.
3. ☐ Tony Bari's wife had enjoyed her holidays in Italy.
4. ☐ Miss Vogel had done some sightseeing in New York.
5. ☐ Tony Bari's wife was envious of Miss Vogel.
6. ☐ Tony Bari's wife did not succeed in removing the smile from Miss Vogel's face.

much. Once it was out in the open, she enjoyed the walking and peace of the countryside, and her husband had been startled and annoyed at how well she adapted to the new situation.

But nobody asked Miss Vogel if she had enjoyed her time when they were away. And if they saw Frank around the place a lot, it was because they assumed he was driving people. Sometimes Miss Vogel wasn't quite as available to baby-sit, walk dogs, listen to problems, arrange flowers. Nothing you could put your finger on. And if she looked happier and walked with a spring in her step and smiled with brighter eyes … they thought she might have lost a few pounds or something.

Tony Bari's wife noticed, however. She had returned from a tedious vacation in Italy with a lot of possessive in-laws and was glad to be back in New York. Her eyes narrowed when Miss Vogel came into the shop. She always suspected Tony Bari harboured feelings for the daughter of the house, and if she had had any money, he would very probably have asked Miss Vogel to marry him.

'Did you have a good vacation, Miss Vogel?' she asked politely, her sharp glance taking in Miss Vogel's improved posture, hairstyle, and general manner.

'Very pleasant, Mrs. Bari. I stayed in New York, got to know my own city. It was delightful.'

Tony Bari's wife, who would love to have done the same, was envious.

'Well, at our age, Miss Vogel, we don't expect very much from vacations, do we?' She was trying to remove the pleased smile from Miss Vogel's face. But she was not succeeding.

Miss Vogel paused in her choosing of expensive mushrooms, specialty cheese, and exotic olive oils and smiled confidently at the woman who had taken away her only hope of marriage and a home, merely because that woman's father had money.

verblüfft • verärgert • zurechtkam

annahmen

Gassi führen • Nichts, was man genau feststellen könnte. • beschwingt

ermüdend • Schwiegerleute

hegte

Blick • Haltung

herrlich

neidisch

entfernen • erfolgreich

selbstsicher • nur

mitfühlend • ihr Beileid aussprechen • Beerdigung • wurde kahl • war faltig • Gier • verlaufen

'Oh, Mrs. Bari, how sad, how very sad to hear you say that,' she said, as deeply sympathetic as if she were offering condolences at a funeral.

Tony Bari was at the other side of the shop. He was fat now and balding, his face set in lines of disappointment and greed. Life had not turned out as he might have wished. How could she ever have thought he would have made her a good husband? Had it all worked out at the time, then she would have just returned from a weary journey to Italy with this bad-tempered man. She would have known no other world but this one; she would never have gone in and out of the lives of the existing people who lived in her building.

wehmütig

She might have looked wistfully at the kind face of Frank, a limousine driver, if she had ever met him, and wondered what it would be like to live in easy companionship with someone who saw beauty everywhere and gain and opportunity nowhere. Tonight, for his birthday, she would cook him a great feast. They had plans for the future, plans young people were making all over the world, but were no less loving and hopeful just because Miss Vogel and Frank were no longer young.

Profit • Festmahl

Übung 5 Welche Satzteile passen zusammen?
Tragen Sie die entsprechenden Buchstaben in die Kästchen ein.

1. ☐ Miss Vogel had come to the delicacies shop

2. ☐ She put the ingredients for Frank's feast

3. ☐ Tony Bari had changed a lot; he was now

4. ☐ Miss Vogel recognised that

5. ☐ People who have a lot of possessions

'Oh, Mrs. Bari,' she repeated, her voice full of genuine sorrow. She had been about to ask, 'What *is* the point of living at all if we don't expect something from every vacation and every day?' but it sounded a bit preachy, and Miss Vogel had learned firsthand from her apartment complex that happiness does not always go hand in hand with having a lot of possessions, so instead she said that to have unrealistic dreams should not be part of the aging process.

And head high, her shopping basket full of exotic ingredients, Miss Vogel left the delicacies shop that had once been her father's bakery and, without a backward glance, walked into the sun-filled streets of New York.

echte Anteilnahme • war im Begriff gewesen • Sinn • moralisierend

Besitz

Älterwerden • Einkaufskorb • Zutaten

a) in her shopping basket.

b) Tony Bari would not have made her a good husband.

c) fat and balding.

d) are not automatically happier than others.

e) because she wanted to buy food for Frank's birthday.

Seven Sisters

It was very odd that they should live in Seven Sisters*, Pat thought for the hundredth time. It seemed too much of a coincidence that anyone who was giving a wife-swapping party, with uninhibited fun and carefree swinging for sophisticated couples, should just happen to live in a place with the group name of Seven Sisters. She had said so to Stuart as well.
'They have to live somewhere,' he said unhelpfully.
Pat had studied the *A to Z*.
'I don't really see why they call it Seven Sisters, it's more Hornsey* really,' she complained.
'If they'd called it Hornsey you'd probably say that that was even more suggestive,' said Stuart mildly.
For two weeks before the party, Pat lived on a high level of anxiety. She examined her new set of underwear with a worried frown. It was red and black, the black bits were

Partnertausch •
hemmungslos •
unbekümmert •
kultiviert
Stadtplan
anzüglich •
sanft •
Unruhe •
Stirnrunzeln

info

Die Einleitung der Kurzgeschichte Seven Sisters spielt mit den Assoziationen, die ihre Hauptpersonen Pat und Stuart mit den Namen zweier Londoner Stadtteile verbinden.

Pat findet es seltsam, dass jemand, der Partnertausch-Partys organisiert, ausgerechnet in einer Gegend lebt, die „sieben Schwestern" heißt – ein Name, der bereits auf größere Gruppen hinweist.

Der Name Hornsey ist sogar noch zweideutiger, denn er klingt fast genauso wie das englische Wort horny mit der Bedeutung „scharf, geil".

Spitze	lace and, in one instance, a rosette. Again and again she tried them on in the bathroom and examined herself critically in the mirror. She looked so very white, and the dark colours made her look almost dead. She wondered
entfachen •	whether this would fire all the men with lust, whether
verrückt	they would be driven insane by the combination of dead white skin, red silk and black lace, or whether one of the
Selbstbräuner	women would take her aside and advise her to use a fake tan lotion. The awful thing was that there was no one to
entsetzlich	ask. Even if she were to write to this appalling magazine where Stuart had first seen the article about wife-swap-
Chiffrenummern	ping and had replied to one of the box numbers, she still wouldn't get a reply in time.
übte	Over and over she rehearsed what she would say: 'Hallo, *lovely* of you to ask us ... what a super house.'
Hure	No, she couldn't tell this terrifying harlot who owned the house in Seven Sisters that it was lovely of her to have invited Pat and Stuart, since Pat and Stuart had in their corrupt and pleasure-seeking way told the
Clique •	Seven Sisters lot that they wanted to come and take off
Haufen •	their clothes to go to bed with a load of strangers. The
ohnmächtig •	more she reminded herself that this is what they had
lächerlich	arranged to do, the more faint and foolish she felt.

Übung 6

Acht englische Begriffe sind in diesem Buchstabendickicht versteckt. Sie sind waagerecht (von links nach rechts), senkrecht (von oben nach unten) oder diagonal (von links oben nach rechts unten) angeordnet.

Die deutschen Entsprechungen der Wörter lauten:

üben	verrückt
Spitze	Kunde
entsetzlich	Durchschnitt
Haufen	lächerlich

Even though she tried to put it from her mind, she wondered if there would be time for any conversation before they got down to action. Would she find herself stark naked in a corner talking to some other naked housewife about the children's drama group or the new supermarket? Would Stuart stand naked laughing with new people about the tomatoes they grew in their allotment?

That was the kind of thing that happened at the ordinary parties they went to … tame little evenings where people kept their clothes on, and didn't mate with each other, and discussed how expensive the season tickets on the train had become, and how hard it was to find a doctor who could spend two minutes listening to you. Tame evenings, dull evenings. Getting in a rut, becoming old before their time, suburban even though they hadn't yet reached their middle-class suburbia, no excitement, nothing very different, nothing that made them gasp.

Two children, the national average, Stuart working in a bank …

God Almighty! – Suppose some of the bank's clients were at the party! It wasn't so ridiculous. People don't

splitternackt
Schrebergarten
harmlos •
sich … begatteten
Trott
ihnen den Atem stocken ließ •
Durchschnitt •
Großer Gott! •
Kunden

b	e	r	i	f	t	e	d	y	s
l	o	s	n	o	i	l	f	w	t
g	i	v	s	o	c	b	t	t	e
a	p	p	a	l	l	i	n	g	y
v	a	u	n	i	i	a	f	s	m
e	l	m	e	s	e	f	c	o	d
r	n	d	l	h	n	o	p	e	r
a	r	t	i	o	t	b	e	l	g
g	r	e	h	e	a	r	s	e	a
e	n	y	t	h	w	d	i	t	s

live beside their banks, some of them could easily live off the Seven Sisters Road. Had Stuart thought of that? She had better tell him, they could call it all off. It would be foolish to imperil his whole career … No. He must have thought of it. He was utterly set on going to this party now. He would only think she was groping around for some excuse.

… nice little flat, no garden unfortunately, but then they went to the allotment at weekends. Children very strong and happy, love their school. Debbie in the school play again this term, and Danny hoping to be picked for the third team. Lots of friends at school always running in and out of the neighbours' houses too and playing in the adventure playground at the end of the road. Not an earth-shaking life, but a happy one … even the school Principal had said the other day …

Sweet God! – Suppose the school ever got to hear of this! How utterly shaming for Debbie and Danny to be branded the children of perverts, sexual freaks. They might even be asked to leave lest their family shame might taint the other children. Relax. How could the school hear of it, unless other parents, or indeed some

neben
sollte es ihm besser sagen • alles abblasen • gefährden • wild entschlossen • suchte
ausgewählt
Abenteuerspielplatz • weltbewegend • Schuldirektor
peinlich • gebrandmarkt • damit nicht • verderben

Übung 7 Vervollständigen Sie die folgenden Sätzen mit den passenden Präpositionen. (at, for, in, of, to, with)

1. Pat and Stuart lived ________ a peaceful community.
2. The adventure playground was ________ the end of the road.
3. Pat and Stuart were aware ________ their children's needs.
4. They made many sacrifices ________ their children.
5. On weekends, Pat, Stuart and their children went ________ their allotment.
6. Stuart talked ________ enthusiasm about his plan.

of the staff, were there being uninhibited and swinging in sophisticated adult fun? ... Yes, of course, if anyone was there, a conspiracy of silence would have to be maintained.
... anyway the school Principal had said that he had enormous admiration for the parents of today, since they made so many sacrifices for their children and were so supportive and aware of all their needs. But he felt sure that this effort was repaid in a thousand ways by the fact that they lived in a peaceful community, far away from the wars and tensions and differences that rend other countries.
Stuart had said that people who went to these parties were normal, ordinary, good, respectable citizens like everyone else. He said that all they were doing was trying to push forward the frontiers of pleasure. They were trying to add to the delights of normal sexual love between a married couple ... and be less selfish about it ... by offering to share that love with other married couples. He had read, and he believed that there was a lot of truth in it, that this kind of generosity, this giving of your rights in your partner to other friends, was an act of love in itself. And, even more important in these treacherous days, it completely by-passed the need to be 'unfaithful' to the other partner – there would be no forbidden lovers, or illicit affairs. It would all be out in the open. It would be healthy and good.
Stuart talked about it with the enthusiasm he had when he first talked about his allotment. His eyes had that gleam that they once had when he had planned a life of self-sufficiency. The rest of London might starve, might poison itself with nuclear fall-out, but Stuart and Pat and Debbie and Danny would grow what they needed for survival on their little allotment, and, aha, who'd laugh then? Pat had asked mildly how Stuart would protect his runner beans and cabbages against twelve million starving Londoners, if they were

Lehrkraft
Verschwörung • aufrechterhalten
Bewunderung • Opfer
Gemeinschaft • Spannungen • spalten
Grenzen • Lust • vergrößern • egoistisch
Großzügigkeit
treulos
verboten • verboten
Glanz • autark • verhungern • radioaktiver Niederschlag • anbauen • Überleben • Stangenbohnen • Kohlköpfe

the only family which had managed to be self-sufficient. Stuart had said it was a technicality.

The Saturday and Sunday gardening continued, it had lost its first flush of real excitement, but nowadays it brought them a gentle pleasure. Perhaps this would happen with wife-swapping too, Pat thought. Soon the heady excitement and flush of enthusiasm would pass, and they would settle into a weekly wife-swap happily and resignedly travelling to Seven Sisters, or Barking, or Rickmansworth, or Biggin Hill.

Stuart seemed so alarmingly calm about it all. This as much as anything disturbed Pat. She had asked him, did he think he should get new jockey-shorts.

'No, love, I've plenty up in the wardrobe,' he had said mystified.

'For the *party*,' she had hissed.

'Why should I need new jockey-shorts?' he had asked, as puzzled as if she had said he should buy a new transistor radio. 'I have nine pairs upstairs. I tell you, I have plenty.'

As the event drew nearer, Pat worried more about Stuart. Did he have no nerves, no feelings, that he could take it all so calmly ... the fact that he had

Hochgefühl

berauschte • sich gewöhnen • ergeben

störte ... am meisten • (eine Art von Unterhose) • Kleiderschrank • überrascht

verwirrt

Übung 8 Ordnen Sie die folgenden Begriffe den drei verschiedenen Wortfeldern zu.

(bar of chocolate, circular saw, gin and lime, hairdryer, jockey shorts, mushroom, negligee, shortbread, skirt, telephone, transistor radio, underwear)

food and drink
(= Essen und Trinken)

______________ ______________

______________ ______________

written to a box number and a woman with a voice like a circular saw had telephoned?

Kreissäge

She had never given too much thought to their sex life. It had always seemed very pleasant and adequate, and she certainly didn't regard herself as frigid, not in the sense of the women's magazine articles on the topic. She couldn't remember saying that she had a headache, or that she didn't feel like it. There was, she supposed, a sort of sameness about it. But then, for heaven's sake, some things *are* the same. The taste of a bar of chocolate or a gin and lime is always the same. The sound of Beethoven's Fifth or Johnny Mathis is always the same. Why this great urge for something different?

keine Lust hatte • Eintönigkeit • um Himmels willen • Schokoriegel • Gin Lemon • Drang

Pat was hurt and puzzled. She had read about women who discovered that their meek and conventional husbands actually liked bondage or violent pornography … so perhaps she should feel relieved that Stuart had suggested only nice old middle-class wife-swapping. Still, Pat felt aggrieved. If she were prepared to live for the rest of their days with their life as it was now, saving for the house, going on a caravan holiday once a year, and making love comfortably in the

lammfromm • Fesselspiele • erleichtert

bedrückt

Wohnwagen

clothes (= Kleidung)	electrical appliances (= Elektrogeräte)
________	________
________	________
________	________
________	________

darkness and privacy of their own room twice a week, then it was somehow ungrateful of Stuart not to feel the same about it.

Pat had an appointment with the hairdresser on the afternoon of the Terrible Day.

'Going somewhere nice?' asked the hairdresser in her bright, routine way.

'Eer … yes,' said Pat.

'Oh, to a function is it?' asked the hairdresser.

'Um. No, no. Not a function. Private house. Old friends, and new friends. A party. An ordinary party,' Pat screamed defensively.

The hairdresser shrugged.

'Very nice, I'm sure,' she said huffily.

The baby-sitter arrived on time. Pat had hoped that she might ring and say she couldn't come. That would mean the end of this ludicrous outing across London to copulate with strangers. The only tingles of excitement she felt were the ones which ran through her brain asking her if she were certifiably insane.

Debbie and Danny barely looked up from the television.

'Goodnight, Mum. Goodnight, Dad. Come in and see us when you get back.'

Pat's eyes filled with tears.

'Stuart love …' she began.

'Goodnight, you lot.' Stuart said firmly.

She had assumed that they would take the car and was startled when Stuart said that it was much simpler than driving to take the tube.

'Only one change,' he said. And to Pat the words seemed sinister and fraught with meaning. She wondered if he was saying that they would only swap with one couple when they got there. She felt nausea rise in her throat. Suppose it were like a dance in the tennis club years ago, when nobody asked you to dance and you ended up grateful for some awful person who eventually did

Termin • Friseur
Veranstaltung
schrie • zuckte mit den Schultern • eingeschnappt • pünktlich • absurd • Prickeln • schoss • völlig • kaum
bestimmt
U-Bahn
unheilvoll • bedeutungsschwanger • Übelkeit

suggest a shuffle around the floor. Could this happen tonight? Suppose some appalling, foul couple rejected by everyone else nodded encouragingly at them? Would they have to say yes? Did the house rules say that there was no opting out?
'Yes, but wouldn't it be nice to have the car coming home?' she asked.
'Mightn't feel like driving on the way back,' said Stuart succinctly.
Worn out with pleasure? Exhausted? Asleep on some strange other wife's bosom? Going home with someone else? Staying with the awful woman in Seven Sisters? What could he mean, he mightn't feel like driving? The whole nightmare was now quite frightening. Why had she ever agreed to this wicked, and silly thing? Why had Stuart ever suggested it?
The tube came immediately, as trains always do when you are going to the dentist or a wife-swapping party. The stations flashed by. Stuart read the back of someone else's evening paper. Pat examined her face three times in her compact mirror.
'You look fine,' Stuart said to her when she got the compact out a fourth time.

Tänzchen • abstoßend • gemieden • nickte … zu • sich zu drücken

kurz angebunden • entkräftet • Erschöpft? • Brust

Albtraum • verrucht

rasten vorüber • begutachtete • Taschenspiegel

Übung 9

Bringen Sie die folgenden Aussagen in die richtige chronologische Reihenfolge und tragen Sie die entsprechenden Nummern in die Kästchen ein.

- ☐ Pat examined herself in her compact mirror.
- ☐ Pat went to the hairdresser.
- ☐ Stuart suggested taking the tube.
- ☐ Pat was embarrassed by the hairdresser's questions.
- ☐ The baby-sitter arrived on time.
- ☐ Pat and Stuart said goodbye to their children.

sowieso 'I suppose you're right. Anyway, it's not my face they'll be looking at,' she said resignedly.

ermutigend 'What? Oh. Oh yes,' said Stuart smiling supportively, and going back to reading the late football results.

'Do you think we'll take off our clothes immediately?'

elend Pat asked wretchedly as they walked out of the station and towards the house.

'I don't know, I expect it depends on whether they have

sachlich central heating,' Stuart said matter of factly.

Pat looked at him as if he were a total stranger.

Andeutung • mit schriller Stimme • Dutzende 'Did she give you any indication of how many people were going to be there?' Pat asked shrilly after another minute of walking. 'I mean, they're not very big houses. They can hardly have dozens.'

'No, she said just a few friends,' said Stuart. 'A few friends, she didn't say how many.'

drängen uns auf • fragte sie mit flehender Stimme • Tränen • rechts abbiegen 'But we're not friends, we're sort of intruding on them in a way aren't we?' she begged. There were tears in her eyes. They were only one corner away from the house now. Right-turn that and they were in the road and there was no going back.

Stuart looked at her, moved by the tears he could hear in her voice.

Übung 10 Vervollständigen Sie die folgenden Sätze, indem Sie das eingeklammerte Verb in die Vergangenheit (simple past) setzen.

1. Pat and Stuart __walked__ (walk) out of the station and towards the house where the party was going to take place.
2. Pat ____________ (ask) Stuart whether she would have to take off her clothes immediately.
3. Stuart ____________ (say) that he didn't know.
4. There ____________ (be) tears in Pat's eyes while they were talking.
5. Pat ____________ (look) at Stuart, her eyes flashing.

'It'll be lovely, Pat dear. You'll love it. You're always a bit nervous at times like this.'

She looked at him, her eyes flashing. — blitzten

'What do you mean at times like this? What "times like this" have there been before? When have we done anything remotely like this. It's the only time like this …' To her horror, she burst into tears. — entfernt

Stuart looked very distressed. He tried to touch her, to put his arm around her, but Pat pushed him away. — beunruhigt

'No, stop saying it's all right, and that I'll love it. I'll hate it. I'm not going. That's final.'

'Well why didn't you say this before? Why did you wait until we're nearly there?' Stuart asked, his innocent, round face looking both foolish and puzzled at the same time. 'I can't understand why you didn't say to me that you thought it wasn't on, then we'd never have set it all up. I thought you wanted to come too.' — unschuldig; dass es nicht drin ist •; ausgemacht •

Pat gave a snort into her tissues. — schnaubte •; Taschentuch

'You *said* it sounded an adventurous thing …' he said.

Pat coughed loudly.

'You *said* we'd try it once and if we didn't like it we'd have got it out of our system,' he went on. — könnten wir das streichen •

Pat blew her nose. — schnäuzte sich

6. She ____________________ (beg) Stuart not to go to the wife-swapping party.

7. Stuart ____________________ (try) to put his arm around Pat, but she wouldn't let him.

8. Pat ____________________ (push) Stuart away.

9. Stuart ____________________ (can) not understand Pat. He was puzzled by her reaction.

10. He ____________________ (think) that Pat also wanted to go to the wife-swapping party.

11. Pat ____________________ (be) very unhappy.

12. She ____________________ (blow) her nose.

'Why, love? Why have you changed your mind now? Just tell me. We'll do whatever you want to. We won't go if you really hate the idea. Just tell me.'

Pat looked at him through her red eyes. His face was indeed very round and innocent. She wondered that she had never noticed that before. He was simply another disappointed young bank clerk. Another man in a dead-end job, with an average wife, a few drinks on a Saturday, two nice, but time-consuming and money-swallowing children, a car that needed a lot of money spent on it, or else needed to be replaced. They had a loan of a caravan each year, but he would never feel the sands of the West Indies or the Seychelles between his toes.

Bankangestellter • ohne Aufstiegschancen • kostspielig • ersetzt • mieteten • die Westindischen Inseln

She began to speak and then stopped. She must be very careful now. It was as if he had been a negative, and now somebody had shown her the developed print. She could see all the frustrations, the hours of commuting, the thickening of his waist. Those things were far from the James Bond or Wild West books he read for a half-hour before he went to sleep each night.

Abzug • Pendeln • Bauchumfang

A surge of understanding went out from her. He just needed some excitement, something out of the ordinary, some proof that he wasn't a mouse, that he was

Welle

Beweis

info

Eine weitere Strategie für das Erschließen unbekannter Wörter ist die Zerlegung in kleinere Bestandteile, die Sie schon kennen. Wenn man zum Beispiel weiß, dass time „Zeit" bedeutet und to consume „verbrauchen", kann man sich ableiten, dass time-consuming „Zeit verbrauchend" ist. Fürs Textverständnis genügt das.

Bei der Übersetzung selbst erschlossener Wörter ins Deutsche ist es jedoch immer sinnvoll, für die im ersten Schritt ermittelte Grobbedeutung im nächsten Schritt ein möglichst treffendes Wort zu suchen. In obigem Beispiel ist dies „zeitraubend" oder „zeitaufwändig".

going to do something daring in his life before he grew old and retired and walked with a stick and crumpled and died.

Quite calmly she looked at him and said:

'I'm jealous. That's it. That's the truth.'

'You're what?' he said.

'I don't want them, to have you, to see you. I don't want those girls to … you know, make free with you. I'd be very jealous. I love you. I don't want them loving you.'

'But Pat,' he said desperately. 'We've been through all this; it's got nothing to do with love. It's got to do with swapping. It's got to do with excitement, and frontiers … and not doing the same things always … till the end of our days.'

She had been right. She resolved that she would do everything her feeble imagination and some sex manuals could dream up if only they got home unscathed from Seven Sisters.

'You're too great,' she said hesitantly. They didn't use flowery endearments, they never paid each other extravagant compliments. It was hard to begin on a street in the middle of the evening in North London on the way to a wife-swapping orgy. But people have to begin somewhere.

'You're too … important. Too precious, and exciting. I love it when we … er … screw. I don't want other women to share it. It's my … er, pleasure.'

'Do you love it?' he asked innocently.

'Oh I do,' she closed her eyes, a sigh of genuine pleasure that she might in fact be going to win escaped her, and it sounded like genuine desire.

'I didn't think you minded all that much one way or another,' he said.

'If you knew how I do,' she said. And then firmly, 'But I wouldn't feel at all the same if you let all these women crawl over you …'

gewagt • verschrumpelte

eifersüchtig

herummachen

verzweifelt

beschloss • schwache Fantasie • Handbücher • unversehrt • zögerlich • blumige Koseworte

Orgie

wertvoll • vögeln

Seufzer • entfuhr • Verlangen

kriechen

She paused. It was a calculated risk. In fact she had given little thought to Stuart's part in the whole sorry business, she had been obsessed with her own role. But she thought that to say this would have been to confirm Stuart in thinking that he had married parochial, puritan riff-raff and that his excitement would be between the covers of books for the rest of his days.

'I often … er … get panicky in case some of the women who come into the bank might … er, proposition you,' she said.

Stuart looked at her.

'There's no need to worry like that. That's kind of paranoid, that jealousy,' he said soothingly. 'I've always been faithful to you. Even this business tonight is *with* you.'

'I don't want to share you with them,' she said. 'I'm not going to. They've got lousy old husbands, awful fellows. I've got you. Why should I be so generous?'

He paused. He looked up the road, he looked down the road. Her eyes never left his face. Down the road won.

'Suppose we got a couple of kebabs …'

'And a bottle of wine.'

traurig • besessen • bestätigen • spießig • Gesindel • bis an sein Lebensende • nervös • anmachen

besänftigend

furchtbar • Kerle

Döner

Übung 11 Ergänzen Sie in den folgenden Sätzen das jeweils passende Wort. (affection, discover, pathetic, sensible)

1. Pat feared that someone could ______________ that she and Stuart were going to a wife-swapping party.
2. She believed that women were more ______________ about sex than men.
3. Stuart recognised how ______________ it might all have been.
4. In a great wave of ______________, Pat realised how much she loved her husband.

As they turned to go back to the station, a middle-aged couple stopped in a car to ask them where the Road was.
Pat asked them what number they wanted.
As she had suspected, it was number 17.
'Have fun,' she said as she gave them directions, and she and Stuart dissolved in laughter.
'They were a bit old,' said Stuart. 'Do you think it would have been very sordid and sort of pathetic?'
Pat wasn't going to let him think that.
'No, there were probably fabulous birds there. Anyway, older ones are more passionate. She'd probably have had you pinned to the hearth rug the moment we got in the door.'
Under a street lamp, she thought his face looked a bit foolish. As if he had seen how tatty and grubby it might all have been. He was very gentle. In a great wave of affection she realised that indeed she would not have liked sharing him with anyone, and that an evening in bed with a bottle of wine, and a nice spicy donar kebab and all that black and red underwear might be the most exciting kind of thing that she had experienced for some time as well.
Women are so much more sensible about sex, she thought cheerfully as Stuart bought the tickets home. She had forgotten the weeks of anxiety, the endless examinations in the mirror, the ceaseless fears lest anyone should discover. Heady with relief she even allowed herself the indulgence of imagining what that elderly woman in the car might look like naked, and she smiled at Stuart who looked like a tiger now that his wife was too rabidly jealous to allow him to indulge in the wife-swapping party to which they had been invited. Horizons had been broadened without anyone having to do anything.

vermutet • den Weg erklärte • brachen in Gelächter aus • schäbig • jämmerlich • tolle Frauen • leidenschaftlich • festgenagelt • Kaminteppich

abgenutzt • schmuddelig • sanft • Welle der Zuneigung • scharf

erlebt

vernünftig

endlos • entdecken • gönnte sie sich

rasend

The Wrong Suitcase

Annie checked in early. She had come out to the airport in plenty of time. None of this was going to be a hassle. Once she had taken her boarding card and seen the smart new case trundle off with its little tag telling it to go to London Heathrow, she sighed with relief; it was all happening now, nothing could stop it. She was going to have the luxury of really looking at the things in the duty-free shop for once, and maybe trying out a few of the perfumes on her wrist. She might even look at cameras and watches – not buy, but look.
Alan was late; he was always late checking in. But he had such a nice smile and looked so genuinely apologetic, nobody seemed to mind. They told him to go straight to the departure gate, and he did – well, more or less. They couldn't expect him to go through that duty-free without buying a bottle of vodka, could

Hektik

schick • Koffer • davonrollen • Anhänger

Handgelenk

zerknirscht • Abflug

Übung 12

Ordnen Sie die folgenden Wörter aus der obigen Textpassage dem ähnlichsten Begriff in der rechten Spalte zu.

hassle	arm
smart	sorry
case	elegant
tag	bother
wrist	label
apologetic	luggage

Verlegenheit

bequem • Business Class • Vielflieger • hatte ... verstaut • Aktenkoffer

they? He had no sign of fuss or confusion; he slipped onto the plane last, but somebody had to come in last. He settled himself easily into his seat in executive class. With the ease of the frequent traveller, he had stowed his briefcase and vodka neatly above, fastened his safety belt in a way that the air hostess could see it was fastened, and he had opened his copy of *Time*. Another business trip begun.

Gepäckband • Sicherheitsbeamte • Zollbeamte • aufschlitzen • versteckt • Überraschungen

U-Bahn • Aufzug

Annie smiled with relief when she saw her case on the carousel at London Airport; she always half expected it to be left behind, like she expected the Special Branch men to call her in and ask her business in England and the Customs men to rip the case apart looking for concealed heroin. She was of a fearful nature, but she knew that and said it wasn't a bad way to be because it led to so many nice surprises when these things didn't happen. She took her case and went unscathed through Customs. She followed the signs for the Underground and got onto a train that she thought must be like a lift in the United Nations building: There were people of every nationality under the sun, and all of their suitcases had different little

Übung 13

Im britischen und im amerikanischen Englisch gibt es einige unterschiedliche Wörter mit derselben Bedeutung. Welche gehören zusammen? Tragen Sie die Buchstaben in die Kästchen ein.

Britisches Englisch

1. ☐ autumn
2. ☐ biscuit
3. ☐ crisps
4. ☐ holiday
5. ☐ lift
6. ☐ motorway
7. ☐ underground

tags. She closed her eyes happily as the train rushed into London. — brauste

Alan reached out easily and took his case as it was about to pass by. He helped a family who couldn't cope with all their cases arriving at once. One by one he swung them off the conveyor belt, and when he took one that wasn't theirs he just swung it easily back again with no fuss. The woman gave him a very grateful smile. Alan had a way of looking better than other people's husbands. He bought an *Evening Standard* in the paper shop and settled himself into a taxi. He had already asked the taxi driver if he could have a receipt at the end of the journey; some of them could be grumpy, always better to say what you want at the start and say it pleasantly. Alan's motto. Alan's secret of success. It was sunset; he looked out briefly at the motorways and the houses with their neat gardens away in the distance. It was nice to be back in London where you didn't know everyone and everyone didn't know you.

fertig wurde mit • Transportband • mürrisch • Sonnenuntergang • Autobahnen

The train took Annie to Gloucester Road, and she walked with a quick and happy step to the hotel, where she had stayed many times. The new suitcase was light

Amerikanisches Englisch

a) highway
b) vacation
c) elevator
d) subway
e) cookie
f) fall
g) potato chips

to carry; it had been expensive, but what the hell – it would last forever. It was so nice, she had bought two of those little suitcase initials and stuck them on. 'A.G.' At first she wondered if this was a dead giveaway, wouldn't people know that they weren't married if they had different initials? But he had laughed at her and patted her nose, telling her that she was a funny little thing and had a fearful nature. And Annie Grant had agreed and remembered that most people didn't give a damn about that sort of thing nowadays. Most people.

getätschelt

scherten sich nicht um

The taxi took Alan to Knightsbridge and the hotel, where they remembered him or pretended to. He always said his name first, just in case. 'Of course, Mr. Green,' the porter said with a smile. 'Good to have you with us again.' Alan folded the receipt from the taxi driver into his wallet and followed the porter to the desk; his room reservation was in order. He made an elegant and flattering remark to the receptionist, which left her patting her hair with pleasure and wondering why the nice ones like Mr. Green didn't ask you out and the yucky ones slobbered all over you. Alan went up to his room and took a bottle of tonic

Brieftasche • Portier • schmeichelhaft

um ein Rendezvous baten • eklig • anmachten

Übung 14 Welche der angegebenen Möglichkeiten ist die richtige? Kreuzen Sie sie bitte an.

1. When Annie opened the suitcase in the hotel, she noticed
- ☐ that it had been damaged.
- ☐ that someone had stolen her camera.
- ☐ that it was not hers.

2. Annie and Alan had picked up each other's suitcases because
- ☐ both suitcases were decorated with the same initials.
- ☐ the taxi drivers had picked up the wrong suitcases.
- ☐ the people at the airport were trying to be funny.

from the minibar. He noticed it wasn't slimline, so he put it back and took soda. Alan was careful about everything.

kalorienreduziert

Annie opened her case in the small hotel bedroom where she would spend one night. She would hang up her dresses to make sure the creases fell out. She would have a bath and use all those nice lotions and bath oils so that they didn't look brand new tomorrow. The key turned and she lifted the lid. There were no dresses and no shoes. Neither the two new nighties nor the very smart toilet bag with its unfamiliar Guerlain products were in the case. There were files and boxes and men's shirts and men's underpants and socks, and more files. Her heart gave several sharp sideways jumps, each one hurting her breastbone. It had happened as she always knew it would happen one day. She had got the wrong case. She looked in terror and there were her initials; somebody else called AG had taken her case. 'Oh my God,' wept Annie Grant, 'oh God, why did you let this happen to me? Why? I'm not *that* bad, God. I'm not hurting anyone else.' Her tears fell into the suitcase.

Falten • sich aushängten

Deckel • Nachthemden • Kulturbeutel • Akten •

hüpfte • Brustbein

Alan opened his case automatically. He would set his papers out on the large table and hang up his suits. Marie always packed perfectly; he had shown her how at an early stage. Poor Marie had once thought you just bundled things in any old how, but, he had explained reasonably, what was the point of her ironing all those shirts so beautifully if they weren't to come out looking as immaculate as they went in? He looked at the top layer of the case in disbelief. Dresses, underwear – female underwear neatly folded. Shoes in plastic bags, a flashy-looking sponge bag with some goo from a chemist in it. God almighty, he had taken the wrong case. But he couldn't have. It had his initials: A.G. He had been thinking that he must get better

hineinstopfte • irgendwie

makellos • Lage

knallig • Kulturbeutel • schmieriges Zeug • Apotheke

ones, these were a bit ordinary. God damn and blast it, why hadn't he got them at the time? For a wild moment he wondered if this was some kind of joke of Marie's; she had been very brooding recently and wanting to come on business trips with him. Could she have packed a case for herself? But that was nonsense; these weren't Marie's things, these belonged to a stranger. Shit, Alan Green said aloud to himself over and over again. What timing. What perfectly bloody timing to lose his case on this of all trips.

It took Annie a tearful seventy minutes on the telephone and many efforts on the part of the airline and of the hotel to prevent her from going out to the airport before she realized that she would have to wait until the next morning. Soothing people in the hotel and in the airline said that it would certainly be returned the following day. She had only discovered an office address for Mr. Bloody Green, typed neatly and taped inside the lid of the case. An office long closed by now.

Tomorrow he would have arrived expecting her to be in fine form and to have her things with her. They were going to go for a week's motoring holiday, the first

- verdammt
- hatte viel gebrütet
- verdammt
- davon abzuhalten
- Büro • getippt • geklebt
- Urlaub mit dem Auto

Übung 15 Welche Satzteile passen zusammen?
Tragen Sie die entsprechenden Buchstaben in die Kästchen ein.

1. ☐ Alan was very angry that

2. ☐ At first Annie wanted to go out to the airport,

3. ☐ The people in the hotel tried to convince Annie

4. ☐ Alan Green's address

5. ☐ Annie was going to go on holiday

time she was going to have him totally to herself. He was flying in from New York and would hire a car at Heathrow; he had told his boss the negotiations would take longer, he had told his wife ... Who knew or cared what he had told his wife? But he would not be best pleased to spend the first day of their holiday in endless negotiations at the airport looking for her things. Was there no way she could find out where this idiot lived? If she phoned his home, even maybe his wife could tell her where he was staying. That was if his wife knew. If wives ever knew.

Verhandlungen

It took Alan five minutes to find the right person, the person who told them that there was no right person at this time of night, but to explain the machinery of the morrow. Yes, fine for those who hadn't arranged a breakfast meeting at seven-thirty A.M., before the shops were open, before he could get a clean shirt. And what was the point of a breakfast meeting without his papers? God rot this stupid woman with her cellophane bags and her tissue paper and her never-worn clothes. Her photograph album, for heaven's sake, and pages and pages of notes, a play of some sort. Hard-to-

das Prozedere des nächsten Tages

zur Hölle mit • Papiertaschentuch • Theaterstück • schwer entzifferbar

a) but then she realised that she would have to wait.

b) was taped inside the lid of the case.

c) with her married lover.

d) that the case would be returned the following day.

e) he had lost his suitcase.

decipher writing, page after bloody page of it. But there was one page where it revealed the address of Miss Prissy A. Grant, whoever she was, and he was sure she *was* a Miss, not a Mrs. A letter addressed to her had 'Ms.'* on it, but Alan had always noted that this was what single, not married, women called themselves. Unfortunately it had no address, or he could have sent for an Irish telephone directory and found her mother and father and got the hotel that their daughter was staying at. That's if she had told them. Nutty kind of girls who carry photograph albums, unworn clothes, and plays written in small cramped writing probably told their families nothing.

enthüllte • brav • sich … bringen lassen • Telefonbuch • verrückt • schwer lesbar

The man who ran the small hotel near Gloucester Road was upset for nice Miss Grant, who often came to spend a night before she went on her long trips to the Continent; she was a teacher, a very polite person always. He took her a pot of tea and some tomato sandwiches in her room. She cried and thanked him as if he had pulled her onto a life raft.

betrieb • Rettungsboot

'Look through his things. You might discover where he is staying,' he advised. Annie was doubtful. Still, as she ate the tomato sandwiches and drained the pot of tea she spread all the papers out on the small bed and read. She read of the plans that Mr. A. Green had been building up over the last two years. Plans which meant that by tomorrow he should be able to take over an agency for himself. If things went the way he hoped.

leerte • breitete … aus • Agentur

Mr. A. Green would return to Dublin at the head of his own company. The arguments were so persuasive that the overseas client would be very foolish not to accept A. Green's offer. There were photocopies of letters marked 'For Your Eyes Only' … there were files with heavy underlining in thick felt pen, 'Do not take to Office.' A great deal of the correspondence was organized so that it showed A. Green's present employ-

Spitze • überzeugend • ausländisch • Unterstreichungen • Filzstift

ers, the people who were paying for this trip to London, in a very poor light. Annie sighed; she supposed that this was the world of business. At school you didn't go plotting against the geography mistress or getting the headmaster to lose confidence in the art teacher. But it seemed a bit sneaky.
Sometimes there were copies of letters his boss *was* shown pinned to those he had *not* been shown. It was masterly filing, and if you read the whole anthology, which up to now had presumably been for Alan Green's eyes only, it made a convincing case. Annie decided that A. Green was a bastard and he deserved to have lost his case and his deal. She hoped he would never find either. But then how would she get back what was hers? And God almighty, suppose he had read her diary.
Alan Green decided to hell with it, he couldn't bear the flat taste of the soda. He opened a calorie-packed tonic water from his minibar and decided that he would do this thing methodically. Look on it as a business problem. He had left his name with the airline, if she called. Of course she would call. Stupid girl, why had she not called already? Stupid A. Grant. She was

in sehr schlechtem Licht • intrigierte • Erdkundelehrerin • Schuldirektor • Vertrauen • hinterhältig • geheftet an

ergab ein überzeugendes Bild • verdiente

Tagebuch

schal • kalorienreich

info

Im Englischen gibt es die Anredeformen

- Mr. (sprich: Mister) für Männer (= dt. Herr)
- Mrs. (sprich: Missis) für verheiratete Frauen (= dt. Frau)
- Miss für unverheiratete Frauen (= dt. Fräulein)
- Ms. (gesprochen wie Miss, aber mit stimmhaftem S am Ende) als neutrale Form für sowohl verheiratete als auch unverheiratete Frauen. Diese Anredeform wird z. B. verwendet, wenn man nicht weiß, ob eine Frau verheiratet ist oder nicht.

probably in a wine bar with an equally stupid teacher talking about plays and how to write them in longhand at great length and maximum stupidity. What kind of play was it, anyway? He began to read it. He read of her romance. … It wasn't a play, it was the real thing. This was a diary. It was more than a diary, it was a plan of campaign. It was dozens of different scenarios that could take place on this holiday.

ausführlich • Schlachtplan

There was the scene where he said he couldn't see her anymore, that his wife had given him an ultimatum. This creepy A. Grant had written out her lines for that one, several times over. Sometimes they were casual and see-if-I-care. Sometimes they were filled with passion, or threats: she would kill herself, let him wait. She had written the whole thing out as if it were a play, even with stage directions.
Alan decided that A. Grant was a raving lunatic and that whoever the poor guy she was going to meet was, he deserved to be warned about her.
He felt glad that she had lost this insane checklist of emotional dramas and how to play them; he was glad that all her finery had gone astray and that

treffen • unheimlich • Text • beiläufig • gleichgültig • Drohungen • Regieanweisungen • völlig verrückt • Kerl • froh • feine Kleidung • verloren gegangen

Übung 16 Kreuzen Sie den Begriff an, der nicht zu den anderen passt.

1. ☐ letter ☐ life raft
   ☐ diary ☐ telephone directory

2. ☐ geography mistress ☐ art teacher
   ☐ headmaster ☐ air hostess

3. ☐ soda ☐ tonic water
   ☐ minibar ☐ gin and lime

she would have to meet the guy as she was. He realized that she had probably done some kind of repair job and washed her tights and whatever just as he had washed the collar and cuffs of his shirt and the soles of his socks. Then he remembered with a lurch that she might have read his dossier on the company.
Annie suddenly remembered she hadn't told the man in the airport where she was staying. She had been too upset. Suppose Mr. Conniving Green had rung in with his whereabouts; they wouldn't have been able to contact her. She telephoned them again. Had Mr. Green called? He had. This was his number. He answered on the second ring. He would come right around with her case. No, please, gentleman's privilege. Very simple mistake, must be a million AGs in the world. He'd come right away.

Kragen • Manschetten • Ruck

hinterhältig • sein Aufenthaltsort

Läuten • Ehrensache

He held the taxi. She was quite pretty, he saw to his surprise, soft and fluffy. He sort of remembered seeing her at London Airport and thinking that if she was in the taxi queue he might suggest they share. Remembering the revelations of her diary, he shuddered with

hielt … auf • flauschig

Warteschlange • schauderte

4.	☐ line	☐ collar
	☐ sole	☐ cuff
5.	☐ creepy	☐ fluffy
	☐ happy	☐ glad
6.	☐ guy	☐ lunatic
	☐ gentleman	☐ ring

relief at his escape. She was surprised to see that he looked so pleasant; she had expected him to look like a fox: sharp-featured, mean pointed little face. He looked normal and nice. She thought she remembered him on the plane up in executive class laughing with the air hostess.

Fuchs • mit scharfen Gesichtszügen • hinterhältig • spitz • Stewardess • unordentlich • mangels • gewühlt

'I have your case here,' she said. 'It's a bit disarrayed, for want of a better word. I was hunting in it to see if I could find out where you were staying.'

'Yours is a little disarrayed too.' He grinned. 'But none of those nice garments of you have fitted me, so they're all safe and sound.'

wohlbehalten

They grinned at each other almost affectionately.

He looked at her for a moment. It was only eleven o'clock at night; in London that meant the evening was only starting. She was quite lovely in a round soft sort of way. …

She wished he didn't have to go. Maybe if she said something about why not go and let's have a bottle of wine to celebrate the found suitcases …

She remembered how he had described his boss as bordering on senility and how he had given chapter and verse to prove that the boss was a heavy drinker.

feiern • an der Grenze zu • genau belegt • ein starker Trinker

Übung 17

Sind die folgenden Aussagen wahr oder falsch?
Tragen Sie ein T für true oder ein F für false in die Kästchen ein.

1. ☐ Alan looked like a fox: sharp-featured and with a mean pointed little face.
2. ☐ Annie was sure she had never seen Alan before in her life.
3. ☐ Alan and Annie excused themselves for looking inside each other's cases.

He remembered how she had proposed threatened suicide with attendant letters to some guy's wife, his children and his colleagues.
They shook hands, and at exactly the same moment they said to each other that they hadn't read each other's papers or anything, and at that moment they both knew that they had.

angedroht • Begleitschreiben

4. ☐ Annie had been hunting in Alan's case to find out what kind of clothes he liked best.

5. ☐ Alan had not read Annie's diary.

6. ☐ For a moment, Alan and Annie thought about going out together.

7. ☐ In the end, Alan and Annie decided not to go out together because they remembered the bad things they had found out when reading each other's secret documents.

Rupert

He bought a packet of mints because Judy Hickey had told him last week that he reeked of garlic and much as she loved all good herby smells she didn't want to sit cooped up beside a porous sponge of garlic for three hours on a small minibus. Funny, Judy: if he had met her in Dublin, he would never have suspected that she came from home. She wasn't a Rathdoon sort of person. He had told her that once and she had retorted that neither was he – a thin, pale, artistic young Protestant: what could be more unlikely?

But she was wrong. There were handfuls of Protestants in every town in the West; they were as much part of the place as the mountains and the phone boxes and the small beautiful churches with hardly any attendance standing dwarfed by the newer Catholic churches which were bursting at the seams. No use

stank • würzig • eingepfercht • ein mit Knoblauch vollgesogener Schwamm • erwidert • blass • künstlerisch

Besucherzahlen • überragt • aus allen Nähten platzten • es brachte nichts

Übung 18

Finden Sie die gesuchten englischen Begriffe mithilfe der Erklärungen und Hinweise. Alle Wörter stehen im Text auf dieser Seite und enthalten den Buchstaben R.

1. a period of sixty minutes _ _ _ r
2. to stink r _ _ _
3. incorrect _ r _ _ _
4. to break open _ _ r _ _
5. a Christian religious building _ _ _ r _ _
6. to reply r _ _ _ r _
7. a cooking ingredient that is similar to an onion _ _ r _ _ _

zigeunerhaft • Pförtnerhäuschen • Einfahrt • Reformhaus

explaining that to Judy, trying to tell her that she was much more unusual, dark and gypsy-like, living in a small gate lodge at the end of the drive from Doon House, growing herbs and working all week in a health food shop in Dublin. In another time she'd have been burned as a witch without any discussion, he had once told her. Judy had said gloomily that the way the country was going it could happen yet, so he shouldn't joke about it.

was … nahe kam

Vorfreude

He smelled of garlic because he had eaten a very good lunch. He always did on a Friday; that was because he wouldn't be back again until late on Sunday night when it was the wrong time to have a meal. So Friday lunchtime was the only opportunity they could get to have anything approaching a relaxed weekend meal before he went back to Rathdoon for the weekend. Of course there *was* the rest of the week but it wasn't quite the same, as there was work next day, and anyway there was something about a weekend that gave you more time – more anticipation. He hated not having his weekends in Dublin. He hated going home on the Lilac Bus.

Zusicherungen • gelüftet • stritt • vergab • tobte • schimpfte • äußerst • fürsorglich • Dankbarkeit

Rupert had never had an argument with his father in his whole life. And he could remember only three differences of opinion with his mother. Those went back to the time he was away at school and she had written three times to the headmaster to receive assurances that the beds were aired. He knew nobody else in the world who had such a relationship with their parents. Everyone else fought and forgave and loved or hated and stormed and railed or became fiercely protective. Nobody had this polite courteous distance based entirely on gratitude and duty. Nobody else who felt such irritation couldn't express it.

Heuchelei

They didn't really need him, that was his whole point, and he wished them well, but he didn't need them either. So why should the pretence be kept up? It made it so much harder on all of them. Not only on Rupert – but maybe it was a little harder on him, he felt, after all their lives were ending. His hadn't really begun and couldn't begin as things were.

There hadn't even been a row when Rupert had decided to give up his law studies. He had been apprenticed to a firm in Dublin, begun his lectures with the Incorporated Law Society and at the same time read for a degree in Trinity. It wasn't superhuman load – a lot of people did it easily – but Rupert never took to it. Not any of it. The bit he liked best oddly was the office. He was quite happy doing the clerical work, the part that Dee Burke, who worked there now said she hated. Rupert had made few friends in Trinity which surprised him; he thought it would be like school, which had been fine. But it was very different and he felt totally outside it all.

He had come home the weekend he knew he had failed his First Law with a heavy heart. He hadn't tried to excuse himself, he just apologised as if to a kind stranger, and his father accepted the apology as if it had been given by a kind stranger. They had sat one on

Streit • hatte als Lehrling begonnen • Vorlesungen • Juristenvereinigung • studierte • (Universität in Dublin) • übermenschlich • Belastung • mochte • Büroarbeit

erstes Juraexamen

Übung 19

Ergänzen Sie die fehlenden Wörter aus den jeweiligen Wortfamilien, die auch im Text auf dieser Doppelseite zu finden sind:

Noun	Verb	Adjective
storm		stormy
protection	to protect	
	to pretend	pretended
	to anticipate	anticipatory
air		airy

either side of the table while his mother looked left and right at whoever was speaking.

Rupert said it was a great waste of his father's money and a disgrace to him in his profession. His father had brushed these things aside: heavens no, people often failed their first examination, there was no cause for alarm, some of the greatest lawyers claimed that they had never been showy scholars. No need for any regrets, it should all be written off as part of sowing wild oats, part of getting your freedom. Next year it would be more serious, head in book, down to it, wasn't that right?

On into the night Rupert had talked, saying that he wasn't cut out for it. It wasn't what he wanted. He didn't believe he would love it when he was in his father's office: he didn't love the office he was apprenticed to in Dublin, he only liked the more mechanical parts. He couldn't get interested in the theory of the law or the way it was administered. He was so sorry it had turned out like this, but wasn't it better that they should know now rather than discover later. They agreed logically that it was. They asked him what DID he want. He didn't know; he had been so sure that he

Schande • beiseitegewischt • Prüfung • behaupteten • Vorzeigestudenten • abgeschrieben • Sich-die-Hörner-Abstoßens • Freiheit • konzentriert • dafür geschaffen

vermittelt

Übung 20

In den folgenden Sätzen fehlen die Bindewörter **either … or** (entweder … oder), **both … and** (sowohl … als auch) oder **neither … nor** (weder … noch).
Setzen Sie die passenden Bindewörter in die Lücken ein.

1. Rupert said that failing his exam was ____________ a waste of money ____________ a disgrace.
2. His father replied that failing an exam was ____________ a cause for alarm ____________ anything to worry about.

would like Trinity, and like studying law, he had never given it much thought before. He liked thinking about the way people lived and their houses and all that. But wasn't it going to be very hard to try and get accepted to study architecture? his father wondered. He didn't mean study it, he didn't know, Rupert said desperately. He would get a job, that's what he'd do. His parents didn't understand this: they thought you had to have a degree to get a job, the kind of job Rupert would want. When he found the position as a junior in the estate agent's they said they were pleased if that's what he wanted. They didn't sound displeased, they sounded remote as they always had been.

His father was remote when he told Rupert that the time had come to get someone else into the office and that if Rupert were absolutely sure that he didn't intend to come into the profession he was going to offer a position to David MacMahon's son. Rupert assured him it would be fine, and got only a minor start when he realised that young MacMahon would have to be offered a partnership and the name of the office would be repainted to read Green and MacMahon. Once or twice they had asked him whether he had

Hochschulabschluss • Juniorstelle • Immobilienagentur • distanziert

beabsichtigte

zuckte … ein wenig zusammen

auf den Namen

3. Rupert's father said that he needed ______________ Rupert ______________ someone else to join him in the office.

4. Rupert liked thinking ______________ about the way people lived ______________ their houses.

5. Rupert's parents expected their son to study ______________ law ______________ some other academic subject.

6. When Rupert told his parents that he was going to work as a junior in an estate agent's, his parents were ______________ pleased ______________ displeased.

thought of coming back to Rathdoon and setting up his own little auctioneering business. There must be plenty of sites being sold and garages and people liked to keep things local. 'It might be no harm to get in before Billy Burns sets one up, he's started everything else in the town,' his mother had said, but firmly and politely he had assured them that this was not going to happen. He left them in no doubt that his plans involved staying in Dublin. This had happened on the day his mother had said that she wondered whether they should put a new roof on the house or not. Sometimes she felt that the one they had would do for their time and wasn't that all it would be needed for ...? Rupert had answered her levelly as if she had been asking no deeper question or making no last desperate plea. He talked of roofs and the value they added to houses and gave the pros and cons as he knew them, bringing himself no more into their plans than if he had been asked by a passing tourist.

Auktionshaus • Grundstücke • nicht schaden • Dach • reichen • ruhig • Bitte • Wert

His mother asked a bit coyly once or twice if he met any nice girls in Dublin. She didn't ask that any more. He must have given her some fairly firm answers,

vorsichtig

info

Bestimmt ist Ihnen schon einmal aufgefallen, dass man manche Wörter immer mit bestimmten anderen Wörtern verwendet. So sagt man zum Beispiel seine Hausaufgaben **machen** und nicht seine Hausaufgaben **tun**. Das klingt im Deutschen komisch. Im Englischen ist es hingegen genau umgekehrt: Hier sagt man to **do** one's homework und verwendet nicht das Wort **make**. Diese sogenannten Kollokationen richtig zu verwenden, ist für Fremdsprachenlerner oft schwer. Doch nur, wenn man Wörter mit passenden anderen Wörtern verwendet, klingt das Ergebnis auch richtig. Daher sollte man sich beim Vokabellernen möglichst auch merken, in welchen Kontexten ein bestimmtes Wort gebraucht wird.

because he was only twenty-five, an age when you might be assumed to be still meeting girls. If people didn't know that you never met girls, you only met Jimmy.

Rupert's throat tightened just thinking of Jimmy. They had met for lunch this Friday; it had now become a bit of a ritual. Jimmy had no classes on a Friday afternoon: they had found the boys didn't study too well and had given them games or art or music. So Jimmy could jump into his little car and drive off to meet him. Rupert had noticed with an alarm mixed with pleasure that Dublin was becoming very slap-happy on Friday afternoons anyway, and not just in schools. At the office they did very little business and people seemed to be leaving for home – even if it was just the suburbs – earlier and earlier. If the noise in a nearby pub was anything to go by those particular workers of the world weren't going to do much to change it when they got back to their desks – if they got back. Still it was nice for Rupert. He could take a long lunch hour with no questions asked. They had found a restaurant that both of them liked (not easy as they had such arguments about food), and it was a very happy couple of hours.
Jimmy insisted that he go home every weekend; it was even Jimmy who found the Lilac Bus for him. Jimmy said it was a pity that they couldn't have weekends but it wouldn't be for ever, and since the old man had always been so undemanding wouldn't it only be right to go back to him now in his last few months? And it must be desperate on his mother waiting all week for him: of course he had to go. Jimmy wouldn't even let him pretend he had flu, not even for one weekend. He was very definite about it.
Jimmy was definite about everything, it was part of his charm. He never wondered about anything or deliberated or weighed things up. And if as it turned

games: Sport
slap-happy: locker
to go by: nach dem man urteilen konnte
undemanding: anspruchslos
definite: unerbittlich •
charm: Charme •
deliberated: dachte nach •
weighed … up: wägte … ab

out sometimes he was utterly wrong, then he was equally definite about that.

'I was all wrong about the man who invented those cats' eyes for the road at night. I was thinking about somebody totally different. I couldn't have been more wrong.' Then he would go ahead with the new view. But he had never changed his view about Rupert going home at weekends; that was an absolute.

Jimmy didn't have any home to go off to on a Friday. Jimmy's home was right there in Dublin. He was the youngest of six, and his two sisters and three brothers had gone exactly the way their father wanted which was into the newspaper vendor business. Some had pitches on good corners, others had roofs over their heads and sold ice creams and birthday cards as well. But Jimmy's father was in the habit of saying gloomily, 'There's always one arty farty cuckoo in the nest, one who won't listen to reason.' Jimmy had been a bit of a pet when he was a youngster: they all encouraged him at his books, and then to university and into teaching in a very posh school. They made jokes about him being gay but it was never said straight out whether they believed he was or not. Anyone over-educated as they regarded him would

weitermachen

Verkäufer • Stände

auf Künstler machend • Vernunft annehmen • Liebling • Kind • vornehm • schwul

Übung 21 Welche Wörter aus dem Text gehören zusammen? Verbinden Sie sie mit einer Linie.

a posh	stick
a vain	house
a crowded	cake
a narrow	coronary arrest
a nice	search
a communal	delicatessen
soggy	school

have had the same abuse, the accusations of being limp-wristed, the mockery of his clothes, the vain search for an ear ring and the camp clichés from the television: 'Ooh Jimmy, you are awful.'

But he went there every Wednesday evening. They all called in on the small crowded house; they talked about rivals and which magazine would be seized by the censor as soon as somebody in authority had a look at it. They talked of how the dailies were doing and how there was no point in taking this magazine because it wouldn't survive to a second issue. They told each other how they had long narrow sticks and beat the hands off any kid stealing a comic. Jimmy would join in by asking questions. He always bought a cake, a big creamy one from the nice delicatessen where they often went. His family would have a communal coronary arrest if they knew how much the cake cost. His mother used to say it was a nice piece of cake even though the smallest bit soggy just in the middle. Jimmy would scoop up the bit where the Cointreau or Calvados had concentrated and eat it with a spoon. His brothers said it was a very fair cake, and reminded them of children's trifle.

Schmähung • schwul • Spott • vergeblich • Tuntenklischees

schauten … vorbei • überfüllt • eingezogen • Tageszeitungen

Auflage • dünn

Feinkostladen • kollektiv • Herzinfarkt

matschig • kratzte zusammen • ordentlich • (eine Art Nachtisch)

Übung 22

Die meisten Wörter haben mehr als nur eine Bedeutung. Ordnen Sie den blau markierten Wörtern die zwei jeweils passenden Bedeutungen zu.

gay	Ausgabe	Grund
pet	ordentlich	Mensch
fair	Mann	hell
man	Vernunft	Haustier
reason	schwul	fröhlich
issue	Liebling	Angelegenheit

It would be so easy to have a family like Jimmy's. They asked so little of him, they were so complete in themselves. If Jimmy were to disappear from their lives for ever, he would be spoken of affectionately, but if Rupert were to forgo just one weekend going home on the Lilac Bus it would be a national crisis for the Green family. Sometimes he thought that this was very unfair, but Jimmy would have none of it.

'You're a difficult sensitive plant, Roopo,' he'd say. 'Even if you had my family, you'd feel threatened and anguished – it's the way things are.'

Rupert would laugh, 'Don't call me Roopo, it sounds like some exotic bird in the zoo.'

'That's what you ARE: like a dark brooding exotic bird that finds almost every climate too difficult for it!'

He had met Jimmy one great lucky day in the office. There was a picture of what they called a 'charming unconverted cottage' in the window. It was a bit far out too, not in the more fashionable direction and it could not be described as trendy, even by the most optimistic of those who wrote the descriptions.

Jimmy came in, a slight figure in an anorak, wearing tinted glasses. He had blonde hair that fell over his forehead and he looked a bit vulnerable. Rupert didn't know why he moved over at once to him even though Miss Kennedy was nearer. He didn't feel any attraction to him at that stage – he just wanted to see that he got a fair deal. He had been studying the picture of the cottage, and had an eager smile on his face.

Rupert had told him the good and the bad: the bad being the roof and the distance and awful boulders of rocks in what had been loosely called the garden. He told him the good, which was that it was fairly cheap, that it was nice and private, and that if you had any money now or later there was another building attached to it which was a sort of an outhouse but which could easily be made into another small dwell-

verzichten
wollte nichts davon hören
gequält
originalbelassen • Häuschen • abgelegen • schick
schlank • getönt • Brille • Stirn • verletzlich
Anziehung
erwartungsvoll
Felsbrocken • sogenannten
Nebengebäude • Wohnhaus

ing. Jimmy listened with growing interest and asked to see it as soon as possible. Rupert drove him out there, and without anything being said they knew they were planning their future as they stood in the wild overgrown rocky ground around the little house and climbed the walls of the outhouse to find that the roof there was perfect.

überwuchert

'It's not handy for where you work,' Rupert pointed out, as Jimmy had said where he taught.

praktisch

'I don't want to live handy to where I work, I want to live miles away, I want to have my own life away from the eyes of the school.'

Rupert felt an unreasonable sense of exclusion.

fühlte sich … ausgeschlossen

'And will you share it, do you think? That is, if you take it,' he had asked.

'I might,' Jimmy had said levelly. 'I have no plans yet.'

He bought the house. He had been saving with a building society for four years and he was considered reliable. The estate agency was pleased with Rupert: they had had the cottage on their books for rather too long. When all the negotiations were over, Rupert felt

Bausparkasse • kreditwürdig befunden

Übung 23

Sowohl since als auch for bedeuten im Deutschen „seit“. Since wird bei Zeitpunkten, for bei Zeitspannen verwendet. Setzen Sie in den folgenden Sätzen das richtige Wort in die Lücke ein.

1. Jimmy had been saving with a building society ____________ four years.

2. The estate agency had been trying to sell the cottage ____________ a long time.

3. Rupert and Jimmy knew they were planning their future ____________ the moment they arrived at the cottage.

4. Rupert had been happy ____________ the day he had met Jimmy.

very lonely. This small smiling Jimmy was going to be off now living his own life in the windswept place. He would build that wall that they had discussed as a shelter, he would do up the second part of the house, paint it white, paint a door bright red maybe, grow some geraniums and get a suitable tenant. It would pay his mortgage. And Rupert would hear no more of it. Or of him.

windig • Schutz • herrichten • geeignet • Hypothek

He phoned on the Friday.

'Rupert, will you help me? I've lost all the fire for the place. I can't SEE it any more, what it's like, what's going to be so great about it. Will you come out and remind me?'

Begeisterung

'Yes.' Rupert said slowly. 'Yes, that's what I'd love to do.'

He sat in a kind of trance all that Friday; if people spoke to him he only heard them vaguely. It was all so clear now: the confusions, the guilt, the hope that it would all settle down and sort itself out and that one day a woman would stuff – which frightened him rather than making him satisfied. But all the time knowing there would be no woman, and not really wanting a woman. But had he read the signs right? Suppose Jimmy was

ungenau • Schuldgefühl • sich … regeln • klären • passen

Übung 24

Welches der angegebenen Wörter passt in die Lücke?

1. Rupert was afraid that Jimmy might have

☐ a fiancée. ☐ debts. ☐ curious neighbours.

2. Jimmy wanted to get a suitable

☐ roof. ☐ gardener. ☐ tenant for his house.

just a charming fellow with nothing on his mind but a good cheery chat with that nice fellow from the estate agent's? Suppose Jimmy said he had a fiancée or some married lady that he wanted to meet in secret. He drove out, noting that it would take him half an hour from door to door should he ever need to go that way again. Jimmy was standing at the gate. Waiting.

He knew it was going to be all right.

And it had been more than all right for three years now. They had done the two little houses up with such love that now they really *did* merit a glowing description on an auctioneer's books. But they would never be for sale. They were separate enough to pretend that they were two dwellings if it were ever needed. But it never was. When Jimmy invited his family out to see the place they all thanked him and said they must get round to it but they never arrived. Rupert didn't press his elderly parents to come to Dublin, and just showed them pictures of his part of the house. And of the garden. They made it all into a giant rockery and knew as much about alpines and rock plants as anyone for miles around. They had a big kitchen with a sink and work area on each side so that they could both cook if

vergnügt • Schwätzchen • Verlobte

verdienten • überschwänglich • zu verkaufen

irgendwann machen

riesig • Steingarten • Gebirgspflanzen • Steinpflanzen • Spülbecken

3. Jimmy wanted to rent the second house in order to pay

- his mortgage.
- for his lunch.
- for his racing car.

4. After doing the two little houses up, Jimmy and Rupert decided that they would never be

- repaired again.
- painted again.
- for sale.

5. Jimmy and Rupert grew

- cucumbers.
- rock plants.
- olive trees in their garden.

they wanted to. Every penny they had went into their little place. They had friends soon, people who came to dinner and admired or offered advice but mainly admired. It was so ideal and they were so happy.

That's why he hated leaving it at weekends. It was on Saturdays that they used to be most peaceful there, often shopping and cooking a meal – not only for Martin and Geoff or other gay friends but for the nice young married couple who lived nearby and who kept an eye on their garden that time they went to Morocco. These were people to relax with. These and one or two people in the estate agency didn't have to have any pretences arranged for them. It was only in Jimmy's school and Rupert's home town that the acting was essential.

Jimmy said it was so ludicrous in the 1980s not to be able to say that he was gay. And he would have at once if it were remotely possible. But no, apparently the boys' parents would think he had designs on them: they would think he was looking at them speculatively.

'I don't want any of those horrible ink-covered filthy ignorant kids,' Jimmy would wail. 'I want you, Rupert, my beautiful dark Rupert that I love.'

Marokko

etwas vorspielen

er habe es auf sie abgesehen • voller Tintenflecken • dreckig • klagte • dunkelhaarig

Übung 25 Aus den Buchstaben des Wortes astounded im Text oben lassen sich viele kürzere Wörter bilden, z. B. as oder tea.
Welche fallen Ihnen noch ein?

____

____

____

info Teachta Dála (Abkürzung: TD) ist die irische Bezeichnung für einen Abgeordneten des Dáil Éireann, des Unterhauses des Parlaments der Republik Irland.

And Rupert would fill up with pleasure and pride that Jimmy could be so natural and open and say all that to him. He tried to say spontaneous things too but they came out with greater difficulty. He was a bit buttoned up as Judy Hickey had once said to him. He wondered often if Judy knew that he was gay. Probably. But it had never been the right time to tell her or to invite her out to see the rock plants and alpines that she would love.

Stolz

zugeknöpft

Of course he could tell Judy Hickey: after all, she was a scandal herself in some way, wasn't she? There had been some really murky business years ago. She would be pleased to know there was another Great Secret in Rathdoon. But he could never tell Judy that one of the real reasons he hated so much leaving every Friday for these empty weekends was that he was so afraid Jimmy would find someone else. Or maybe even had found someone else.

undurchsichtig

At lunch this very Friday he had asked Jimmy what he would do all day Saturday, and there had been no satisfactory answer. Martin and Geoff were having people in for drinks – he would go to that in the evening. He'd mark exercise books, he'd try and fix up the hi-fi which had never been satisfactory. It was all very vague. Suppose, suppose, Jimmy had begun to like somebody else? His heart was cold inside like the unexpected bit you find when you take a loaf out of the freezer and it hasn't properly thawed. He could never tell anyone that fear. Not anyone in the whole world.

zufriedenstellend • hatten Besuch

benoten • Schulhefte • reparieren

Laib Brot • Gefrierfach • aufgetaut

It was easy to talk to Judy. She told him about her little herb pillows; he told her all the fuss over the TD* with the love nest. They both laughed at that and for some reason that he couldn't quite see it brought her into talking about her own past. He was astounded at her story, a young wife and mother dealing in drugs all those years ago. And the husband doing deals with the law as if he was part of the Wild West. Imagine her not seeing the children, but imagine even more her getting

Kräuterkissen • Abgeordneter

erstaunt

supplies of LSD for the huntin' shootin' fishin' set! And hash! Jimmy would go wild when he heard. He could have listened for ever but suddenly she decided she was boring him and launched into chat with that half-mad Nancy Morris. She had also said that his mother thought about him every day. That couldn't be so. Mother thought about father, and the house, and the vegetable garden and the hens, but mainly father and how she was afraid that young Mr MacMahon didn't have the respect due to the senior partner and founder of the firm. Mother hardly showed any interest in Rupert's life in Dublin which was of course a relief, but it did mean that it was most unlikely that Mother would think about him every day. Surely Judy was being fanciful? She probably hoped no matter what she said her lost children thought of her every day. That was it.

Their house was small and white with clematis growing up over the porch. Jimmy thought that a Protestant solicitor's family would live in a manor house, heavy with creeper and inspiring awe among the peasantry. Rupert had said that only two houses had proper creeper. One was Dr Burke's, which was beautifully

Lieferungen • bessere Gesellschaft • durchdrehen • langweilte • begann

Hühner

den ... verdiente • Gründer

übertrieb • egal

Klematis • Vordach • Anwalt • Herrenhaus • voller Kletterpflanzen • Ehrfurcht erregend • Bauern

Übung 26 Die folgenden Wörter bedeuten das Gegenteil von Wörtern auf dieser Doppelseite. Tragen Sie die gesuchten Wörter ein.

1. black ____________________
2. mother ____________________
3. interesting ____________________
4. tiny ____________________
5. light (n) ____________________
6. adult (n) ____________________
7. large ____________________

kept and one was the old vicarage, which was so neglected it now looked like a huge stone covered with ivy. They had a service each Sunday in Rathdoon in the beautiful church, but had no vicar, no rector; he came out from the big town seventeen miles away and had Matins in Rathdoon, and another, later Matins another fifteen miles down the road. Jimmy was fascinated, but Rupert had never asked Jimmy home to meet the family. Jimmy had asked him to his house many a time. Rupert had gone once and felt awkward even though nobody else had and they had all buttonholed him about the price of property.

His mother was waiting just inside the door. That always annoyed him too and he got annoyed with himself over the very annoyance. Why shouldn't she wait to stop him ringing or knocking and disturbing his father's sleep. But it always made him think she had been standing waiting for his shadow to fall through the glass panels. He said goodnight with a much lighter tone than he felt, and braced himself. The soft leather of the magnificent jacket touched the back of his neck. It was Jimmy's birthday present to him. A few days early but Jimmy said it would cheer

Pfarrhaus • vernachlässigt • riesig • Efeu • Gottesdienst • Pfarrer • Pfarrer • Frühgottesdienst

unwohl • gelöchert

Schatten • Scheiben • riss sich zusammen • wundervoll • aufmuntern

Übung 27

In den folgenden Wörtern von dieser Doppelseite fehlen insgesamt drei verschiedene Buchstaben. Welche sind das, und welches Wort kann man daraus bilden?

_ w k w _ r d
b o r i n _
i v _
m _ _ n i f i c e w n t
p e _ s _ n t r _
v i c _ r _ _ e

him up for the weekend. Dee Burke had been right, they did cost a fortune. Again the niggling worry: how had Jimmy been able to spend that much money even if it was a second? Put these doubts away, Rupert, he told himself firmly. Jimmy is good and true. Why pour vinegar onto it all with your stupid suspicions. Jimmy is at home tonight marking books and looking at television, Jimmy is not in a bar in town cruising someone. Why destroy EVERYTHING?

'He's very well, very clear,' his mother whispered delightedly.

'What?'

'Your father. He's very clear. He's awake; he asked several times what time would the Lilac Bus be in. Every time he heard anything change gear on the corner, he said 'Is that the bus?''

Rupert put his carrier bag down on the hall floor. 'That's great Mother, that's really great,' he said with heavy heart and went up the little stairs slowly to see the man with the head like a skull and the skin like cling-film. The man he had never been able to talk to in his life.

It was a sunny Saturday but his father's room was darkened and the dim light hurt his eyes. His mother was bottling fruit downstairs. Jimmy said Catholics never bottled fruit or preserved eggs – it was something their religion didn't go along with. Jimmy had told him more lies about Roman Catholicism than he ever believed anyone could invent. He had always been brought up carefully to respect it at a distance by his parents, and even though they thought it definitely held the people back they were impressed by the piety and the crowds going to Mass. His parents had gone to Galway to see the Pope. Jimmy said that his parents had made a small fortune the weekend the Pope arrived since the whole of Dublin wanted to buy every newspaper twice in case they missed anything.

Vermögen • nagend • zweite Wahl • lieb • treu • verdirbst du es und reißt ... auf • zerstören • flüsterte

ankommen • den Gang wechseln

Totenschädel • Frischhaltefolie

dämmrig • machte ... ein • einlegten • mit dem ... sich nicht vertrug • sich ausdenken • erzogen

beeindruckt • Frömmigkeit • Papst

Back at home in the cottage, Jimmy would be drinking freshly brewed coffee and reading the *Irish Times*. Then he might go out to the garden and do some transplanting: September was the month to move the evergreens if you wanted to change the plan a bit. But no, Jimmy would wait for him to come back for that. Maybe he would be puzzling over the hi-fi. Please may he not be driving into town just because he's bored; please may he meet nobody at lunch over a drink and smoked salmon sandwich.

gekocht
Umpflanzen • immergrüne Pflanzen • grübeln
Räucherlachs

'You're very good to come down every weekend,' his mother said suddenly as if she could read the home-sickness for his real place written all over his eyes. 'Your father really does like talking to you. Do you notice that? Can you see it?'

plötzlich • Heimweh

Jimmy had begged him not to cross the whole of Ireland and then have a row. How could Jimmy understand that there were NEVER rows, and there never would be. Well, a coldness then, Jimmy would say. If you are going to go to all that trouble, it's silly to balls up your weekend: if you're making the gesture, make it properly.

durchqueren
vermasseln

'I think he *does* seem to like talking,' Rupert said. 'It doesn't tire him too much, does it?'

Übung 28

Welche der folgenden Adjektive beschreiben Jimmy? Kreuzen Sie sie an.

- ☐ good
- ☐ anguished
- ☐ gay
- ☐ remote
- ☐ reliable
- ☐ gypsy-like
- ☐ true

'No, he plans all week what he's going to say to you. Sometimes he asks me to write it down, or just headings. I want to talk to Rupert about this, he'll say, and I write it down. Often he forgets what it was he was going to say about it, but it's there at the time.'

Stichpunkte

Rupert nodded glumly.

finster

'Like he was going to ask you about those flats you sell in blocks: he was very interested in how they work out the leasehold. He said that there was never any of that in the conveyancing he had to do. But all he asked me to write down was 'Block of Flats,' you see, and then he couldn't remember last week what it was he wanted to say about them.'

en bloc • Pacht • Eigentums-übertragungen

'I see,' Rupert said, trying to sound more sympathetic than he was afraid he might appear.

'But this week, he seems very much brighter and more aware, doesn't he?' she was pleading.

wacher • sagte sie bittend

'Yes, much more. Oh indeed. He was talking about this house here and what we would say if we had it on an auctioneer's book. I was giving him funny descriptions and he smiled a bit at it.'

Rupert's mother was pleased. 'Good, he hasn't smiled a lot. That's nice.'

Übung 29 Welche Satzteile passen zusammen?
Tragen Sie die entsprechenden Buchstaben in die Kästchen ein.

1. ☐ Rupert's father planned all week

2. ☐ Rupert's mother was very happy to hear

3. ☐ Rupert suggested to his mother

4. ☐ But his mother

5. ☐ Rupert was appalled

'Why don't you have a bit of time off, Mother, when I'm here. Why can't you go into town, maybe, you'd like that. I can keep an eye on father and be here if he wants anything.'
'No no, I want you to enjoy yourself,' she said.
'But really Mother, I mean I'm not doing anything anyway.' He shrugged. 'I might as well look after father and let you have a few hours to yourself.' He meant it generously, but he knew it had come out all wrong.
'But you're home for the weekend,' she cried. 'I wouldn't want to miss that by going off the town. I can do that any day: Mrs Morris or young Mary Burns, Billy's wife, would sit with him. No, I want to get value out of your being here.'
'Sure. Of course,' he said, appalled at his own insensitivity. Jimmy would never in a million years have said anything like that. Jimmy would have brought life and laughter into the house the moment he got back. Jimmy. Oh Jimmy.
They had lunch, the kind of lunch that only his mother could serve: endless preparation and toasting of bread and cutting of crusts and spreading of cheese and slicing of tomatoes. And yet it was nothing – it man-

nimmst … dir … Zeit für dich • ein Auge auf … haben

kann ebenso gut

rief

etwas davon haben • entsetzt • Mangel an Einfühlsamkeit

In-Scheiben-Schneiden

a) at his own insensitivity.

b) to have a bit of time off.

c) what he was going to say to his son.

d) that her husband had smiled at Rupert's funny descriptions.

e) wanted to get value out of her son being home.

aged to be both stodgy and insubstantial. If only she would let him cook. But then he had never asked her. Perhaps it might be giving something away to say that he could have made them a light and delicious lunch in a quarter the time. It was his own fault like everything. His father struggled all afternoon. And Rupert struggled back.

Sometimes his mother was there, sewing. She was always making little things for her sister who was married to a vicar and who always needed things for parish sales. His father would struggle and concentrate. His efforts to please meant that he could even be re-routed back to his own old days as a solicitor coming first to the town, when things were different and better. There was a time when his father had been happy to ramble through the times gone by. But not now: it was as if he was determined to show a guest in his eyes that he *was* interested in whatever kind of strange thing the guest did for a living. All afternoon Rupert's soul was crying out, 'It's all RIGHT father. Look, can't you rest: I have an okay life and I wish you and mother well but why do we go through all this meaningless chat. There is nothing to say any more.'

schwer verdaulich • nicht sättigend • etwas verraten

mühte sich … ab

Kirchenbasare

es recht zu machen • umgelenkt • durch … zu streifen • fest entschlossen • beruflich machte • Seele • ausruhen

Übung 30

Ersetzen Sie die blau markierten Wörter in den folgenden Sätzen durch bedeutungsähnliche Wörter oder Ausdrücke von dieser Doppelseite.

1. Rupert's father made an effort all afternoon.
2. Rupert's aunt always needed things for church bazaars.
3. Rupert's father had been happy to remember the times gone by.
4. Now he really wanted to show his son that he was interested in his job.
5. Rupert wanted his father to relax.
6. Judy Hickey held her head high for twenty years.

The sun was almost going down when he could bear it no more; he said he had promised Judy Hickey he would do something for her and he had better dash over to her.
'A brave woman, Judy Hickey – she held her head high in this place for two decades,' his father said in a surprisingly strong voice.' 'Yes, well, why not?' Rupert was defensive. 'She got a harsh punishment.'
'She took it, and she didn't run away and hide. She stepped down from being lady of the manor and lived in the gate lodge.'
'And lost her children,' Rupert's mother added. 'That was the worst bit.'
'Yes, well, I won't be long.' He felt he could breathe again when he was out in the air; he left the square and went off towards the gate lodge of the big Doon house.
Judy was lying curled up like a cat. She wasn't pleased to see him – in fact she nearly sent him back straight away. She was like Jimmy really but without the persuasive charm: Jimmy made it seem reasonable; Judy made it seem like a duty.
But she meant it: she got up and stretched and said she was going to go out and walk in her husband's wood. Jack Hickey's wood she called it. She said he should talk about anything, anything to show his father that he was trying too.
But what could he say? He couldn't tell him that his heart was tearing with the barbed wire of jealousy in case his male lover might have been unfaithful. Then NOBODY could tell a father that about a lover of any sex. But Rupert was worse off: he couldn't talk about his life, about the beautiful gentians that he and Jimmy had planted and how the willow gentian had burst into a whole pool of dark blue flowers last July and they had taken photographs of each other admiring it. He found it hard to talk about the garden without mentioning Jimmy because the two were twined

bear: ertragen
dash over: rübersausen
brave: mutig • decades: Jahrzehnte • voice: Stimme • harsh punishment: harte Strafe • hide: sich versteckt • stepped down: ist abgestiegen
be long: lange brauchen
curled up: zusammengerollt
stretched: streckte sich
was tearing: zerriss • barbed wire: Stacheldraht • male: männlich • worse off: schlechter dran • gentians: Enziane • willow gentian: Schwalbenwurzenzian • burst: sich rasend ausgebreitet hatte • pool: Teppich • twined: verknüpft

together, like the house, like cooking, like holidays and reading and laughing and the things people did for heaven's sake.

kurz angebunden — Annoyed with Judy for being short with him, he walked home. He passed the Kennedy's shop and saw a big hereingeführt — handsome girl being ushered in. The red-headed Kennedy boy, Eddie, was looking at her with a foolish miteinander gehen — grin: they must be courting. She was very attractive; how simple life would have been if only he had been born to court a big handsome girl who would bring life and laughter into his quiet house.

Suddenly he thought of Jimmy in the house. Jimmy mit den Händen umfasste — pausing at the door to touch the clematis and cup it in his hands with admiration. Jimmy saying to Rupert's mother that she should sit down and put her feet up hässlich • zur Abwechslung • — and let her big ugly son and himself make the meal for a change. Jimmy telling Rupert's father tales of the Schulgebühren • Zuschläge — boys' school where he taught, and the fees and the extras and the awful school concerts. Jimmy walking casually down the road with him to Ryan's for a drink Rostbraten • drall • wohlhabend — before dinner while the carbonade was in the oven. Jimmy would lighten their house better than any strapping girl from a well-to-do farm outside town.

Übung 31 Die folgenden Wörter bedeuten das Gegenteil von Wörtern auf dieser Doppelseite. Tragen Sie die gesuchten Wörter ein.

1. bad ____________________
2. stand up ____________________
3. beautiful ____________________
4. boring ____________________
5. foot ____________________
6. separated ____________________
7. boy ____________________

'I was just thinking,' he said to his mother when she let him in the door again as if she had been hovering. 'Could I bring a friend home next weekend?'

herumgestanden

After that it was easy. His mother said she was glad that she had got good notice because she would clear out the guest room. It had been something she had meant to do for a long time but never had the heart somehow. And his father said that it would be very interesting to meet someone who taught in that school because he had known a lot of people in his time who had been there and they were all united in never having a good word to say for it but having done extremely well as a result of being there.

frühzeitig erfahren • ausräumen • vorhatte • übers Herz gebracht hatte • irgendwie

einig

Then a sudden shock. Suppose Jimmy didn't want to come?
'I hope he'll be able to make it; I didn't think of asking him,' he stammered.
'Why don't you ring him?' his mother suggested. His mother. Who made trunk calls as one might try to get in touch with another planet. Cautiously and without much hope of success.
'God, isn't that lovely to hear you?' Jimmy said.
'I'm ringing from home,' said Rupert.
'Well, I hope so. I did think sometimes you went off to exotic places without me, but I decided to trust you.'
Jimmy's laugh was warm. Rupert swallowed.
'It's lovely here this weekend and I was wondering … I was wondering …'
'Yes?'
'I was wondering if you'd like to come down next week and stay, you know?'
'I'd love to.'
There was a pause.
'You would? You would, Jimmy?'
'Sure I thought you'd never ask,' Jimmy said.

es schaffen • stammelte • Ferngespräche • mit … Kontakt aufzunehmen • vorsichtig

schluckte

ich dachte schon

The Business Trip

Lena had loved him for four long years. Not that he knew, of course. Men like Shay wouldn't even consider that they could be loved silently and unselfishly like that. It didn't make sense.
He probably assumed that Lena was fond of him, admired him, and might under the right circumstances be attracted to him. But if he thought of her at all, he might have assumed that she had a private life of her own. He would never have thought that this quiet, efficient assistant of his spent her entire life, both in and out of the office, thinking about him, trying to make his life easier and better, and in her dreams trying to share that life with him.
According to Maggie, Lena was not in love. She was suffering from an obsession, an infatuation. It wasn't healthy for someone who was twenty-six to develop

auf die Idee kommen • still • selbstlos • mochte • Umstände

ganz

fixe Idee • Schwärmerei

Welche der folgenden Adjektive beschreiben Lena? Kreuzen Sie sie an.

Übung 32

- [ ] unselfish
- [ ] loud
- [ ] efficient
- [ ] self-confident
- [ ] obsessive

Schwärmerei • vorübergehend • sich breit zu machen • wirklich • vorweisen • lebhaft • sich öffentlich zum Narren gemacht • sich mit dem Zweitbesten zufriedengegeben • geschätzt • Mitleid • „na, na“ sagen • Verbündete • trennten

this kind of crush on a man who didn't return it and wasn't even aware of it. And however unwise it might have been to have allowed a temporary fascination to take over, it was positively dangerous to let it continue the way Lena had. She stopped being twenty-six and became twenty-seven, and twenty-eight and twenty-nine. Soon she would be thirty years of age, and what had she to show for it?

Lena said spiritedly that she had as much to show for it as anyone had to show for anything. She had been happy, she had made his life better. She hadn't made a public fool of herself, as so many women had. She hadn't settled for second best, as so many others had done. She loved every second of her working day, which was more than you could say for a lot of people. She was appreciated if not loved in her office, and only Maggie knew her secret. She was not an object of pity. Maggie wouldn't tut-tut and shake her head over coffee with the girls about Lena's foolishness. Maggie was an ally, even if she didn't understand.

Maggie was Lena's aunt. But they had always been much more like cousins or sisters. Only ten years divided them in age, and the teenage Maggie had loved

Übung 33

Beantworten Sie die folgenden Fragen, indem Sie die richtigen Antworten – also evtl. auch mehr als eine pro Frage – ankreuzen.

1. Does Shay love Lena?

- ☐ Yes, he has loved her for four years.
- ☐ No, he does not even like her.
- ☐ We do not know; and he does not know that Lena loves him.

2. Does Lena love Shay?

- ☐ No, she hates him because he has hurt her feelings.
- ☐ Lena is convinced that she loves Shay.
- ☐ Maggie believes that Lena does not really love Shay.

the toddler, Lena, and treated her as a friend. Now Maggie, almost forty, with huge dark eyes and a great mane of black curly hair, looked and acted younger than her niece. Her life was fuller by far. Maggie's problem had never been making men love her. It had been trying to stop them from loving her unwisely. And sometimes trying to stop herself from loving them in return – equally unwisely.

She had been married twice, widowed the first time, separated the second time, but these were only small milestones in the list of Maggie's love: sensible married men, fathers of large and settled families, wanted to throw up everything and move in with Maggie. She often had great trouble persuading them to do nothing of the sort. It wasn't that she gave them unmentionable sexual favors, she told Lena with her big dark eyes full of honesty, it was just that they saw, however foolishly, a kind of life with her where they wouldn't be hassled and troubled. They saw a strange and unrealistic freedom in living with Maggie, something they didn't have at home. Maggie would never ask them to come to the supermarket and push the trolley, Maggie wasn't a one for wanting the grass cut or the house painted, the car

Kleinkind

Mähne • lockig

zurück • verwitwet

gestanden • hinschmeißen • mit … zusammenziehen • zu überzeugen • dergleichen • unaussprechlich • belästigt

den Einkaufswagen schieben

3. Why does Maggie tell Lena that she should stop being obsessed with Shay?

- ☐ Because Lena is almost thirty years old and should rather start a real relationship with a man.
- ☐ Because Shay is actually a murderer.
- ☐ Because Maggie is in love with Shay herself.

4. Why does Lena protest that she is happy with her life?

- ☐ Because she has not settled for second best, like many others.
- ☐ Because she loves every second of her working day.
- ☐ Because she is appreciated in her office.

Veranda	cleaned or the patio built up to impress the neighbors.
	Maggie would be happy to eat a meal of wild mushrooms
Erdbeeren •	and brown bread followed by strawberries. Very far from
energisch	real life. Maggie would agree with them fervently that
	she was indeed far from real life and they must see her
ab und zu •	only now and then. The more she protested, the more
empört	they wanted her. Lena said she was outraged at the way
	Maggie got every man she wanted, and yet she, Lena,
einhielt	who kept all the rules, couldn't get just the one.
	Lena did keep the rules as written in the women's
glänzend	magazines. She had shiny, well-cut hair, she was tall
	and slim, she had been to makeup lessons to make the
Teint • hell	most of her good complexion, her fair skin, and blue
	eyes. She dressed well and kept her clothes immacu-
schimpfte	lately. Well, why wouldn't she, Maggie grumbled, if she
	stayed at home every evening dreaming of lover boy
	Shay. There was all the time in the world to iron her
polieren •	blouses and sponge her skirts and polish her shoes,
Gürtel •	handbags, and belts till they shone. But had it done
Abteilung	one bit of good in the department where she wanted it
	to succeed? No. None at all.
	Lena's friends and colleagues all said she looked very
Lob	smart, but their praise and admiration was of no

Übung 34 Welche Aussagen über Lena stimmen? Kreuzen Sie sie an.

- [ ] She has shiny, well-cut hair.
- [ ] Her eyes are a dark brown.
- [ ] She is slim but not tall.
- [ ] She knows how to make the most of her fair complexion.
- [ ] She can get every man she wants.
- [ ] Her thirtieth birthday is coming up.
- [ ] Her favourite foods are wild mushrooms, brown bread and strawberries.

interest to her. Sometimes they wondered why she didn't have a man in her life. She put them off with a laugh. And apart from Maggie, nobody had an inkling. Maggie's grumbling had always been good-natured. But now it was different. Two things were coming up: Lena's thirtieth birthday, and a business trip with the famous Shay. Yes, he had asked the loyal Lena to London with him. Driving in his car, for a whole week.	wehrte … ab • hatte … die leiseste Ahnung • freundlich • rückten näher
Maggie felt it was time to play the heavy aunt for the first time in her life. She sat Lena down and told her to get ready for a serious lecture.	als Tante ein Machtwort zu sprechen
'Oh, not now,' Lena had cried. 'Not now. There's so much to be done, so many preparations. I have to decide what to wear, what to say, what social plans to set up, as well as all his business meetings. Can't the lecture wait till I get home?'	Freizeitunternehmungen
'No, it can't.' Maggie was adamant. 'It's about the trip; this has to be the make-or-break time. When you come back on the ferry and drive off the ramp, Shay must either be involved with you properly or else you will have given up all notion of him.'	unnachgiebig • entscheidend • Rampe • zusammen • aus dem Kopf geschlagen
Lena's blue eyes filled with tears. 'I don't want anything as definite, as black-and-white, as that. Why does it all have to hinge on this trip?' She looked appalled at having to abandon what was after all the central part of her life.	abhängen von • aufgeben
'Because you are leaving your twenties and for the first time you are leaving the country with his beauty, and you have the rest of your life ahead of you.'	vor •
'It's too frightening. I don't want to try and seduce him or something like that.' Lena was trembling at the thought.	verführen • zitterte
'Well, what's all the fuss about what you're going to wear and how you're going to look? If you don't want him to fancy you, why don't you just go in an old sweater and a pair of jeans?' Maggie was ruthless.	auf dich steht • unbarmherzig

'It's different for you, you can make anyone fancy you.'

Mühe gäbst • 'So could you if you bothered. It's got nothing to
auftragen • do with well-cut jackets and applying your blusher
Rouge properly,' Maggie said.

'How, then?' Lena was eager.

'I'll tell you, but only if you promise me that you will decide one way or another at the end of the week. When you come back off that car ferry, you'll either be involved with him properly as two normal people who love each other, or you will leave that job, and put him out of your mind and heart.'

Teufel 'It's like doing a deal with the devil,' Lena complained.

Schutzengel 'Much more like a guardian angel,' Maggie said.

They sat for three hours, Maggie with her notebook. At no stage were outfits or perfumes mentioned. There was no strategy about booking one room by mistake
Suche • instead of two. There was to be no research into roman-
schummrig • tic restaurants in London where the lights would be
Hintergrund • low and there might even be violins in the background.
lachhafte No, if Lena was to get her man these kinds of cheap
Versuche tricks were only Mickey Mouse efforts, according to

Übung 35 Tragen Sie die gesuchten Begriffe in das Kreuzworträtsel ein.

1. makeup that women use to make their cheeks red
2. your brother or sister's son
3. a place where you go to wash your clothes
4. to put on
5. the opposite of patience
6. the activity of looking for information
7. a higher being
8. a series
9. your brother or sister's daughter
10. to make an effort

Maggie. And since almost every man who moved in Dublin seemed to fancy Maggie in some way or other, she was worth listening to.

Maggie seemed shocked that Lena had worked for this man for four years, not to mention thinking that she had loved him for this length of time, and still knew so little about him. Maggie asked a string of questions. Lena knew nothing about his school days, whether he had liked it there or not, and how he had got into the business world in the first place. She didn't know who his first employers had been, whether he had found it easy or frightening. She didn't know what television programs he watched, and when he went to a match if it was because he knew all about the game or because he liked the sociability of it. Lena didn't know how he got on with his two brothers and sister, how often he went to see his mother. She didn't know if he liked being with his nephews and nieces. If he felt lonely on weekends, as so many people did in Dublin. How he decided what to eat and whether he had a washing machine or went to the launderette.

'What *do* you know about him, for heaven's sake?' Maggie asked with some impatience.

string – Reihe
sociability – Geselligkeit
got on – sich … verstand
nephews – Neffen
nieces – Nichten
launderette – Waschsalon
impatience – Ungeduld

1	L
2	E
3	N
4	A
	&
5	M
6	A
7	G
8	G
9	I
10	E

gegenwärtig Lena knew all about his current and past girlfriends, and she knew the restaurants he went to, and the nightclubs, and the bills for bouquets of flowers. She knew that and she knew about him at work, where he was tough and not afraid to go into a meeting and fight.

gut informiert 'Well-briefed by you, of course, with reports you have been working on all weekend when you weren't putting more henna in your hair, hoping he'd notice.'

'I love him,' protested Lena.

'No, you don't love him at all. You don't know the first thing about him apart from this empty social thing. You might love him when you get to know him, and he might love you. But you might find him empty.'

Lena refused to accept this but agreed meekly to follow Maggie's advice. In the ship's dining room over a meal she would begin, and in the long drive across Britain she would not veer between business talk and gossip-column chat about nightclubs she didn't even know. She would talk to him about himself.

wechseln • Klatsch

'Suppose he asks me about myself?' Lena asked fearfully.

Maggie didn't much think he would, but if he did, then she was to tell him the truth. Say she was perfectly happy, she had no wish to change from her life the way it was, assure him it was satisfactory. There was nothing that drove men as mad as that – the thought that women were actually contented the way they were, not scheming and conniving.

verrückt machte • zufrieden • hinterhältig • durchtrieben

'But that's not strictly true. I'm not totally contented the way I am,' Lena complained.

• ganz

Maggie shrugged. 'You always tell me you are when I try to change you.'

It was unanswerable.

The day before the trip Maggie rang her to wish her luck. 'One thing, Lena, and remember this: He will notice you, he will fancy you. Truthfully, but you may not fancy him.'

'I probably gave you much too shallow a view of him,' Lena whispered in case anyone in the office would hear. — oberflächlich

'If that was your view of him after four years of loving him, then I'm sure what you told me was very accurate,' Maggie said.

Lena learned a lot that night at dinner on board ship. She learned that his mother was demanding and never satisfied, that his brothers were discontented and jealous of his success. She heard that Shay's sisters didn't know how to bring up their children properly and gave in to them in everything. She heard that his school was full of sadistic teachers and moronic pupils, that they had ripped him off in his first job and cheated him in his second, and he had seen them coming in his third. He liked to cook but not to wash up; he thought these service apartments he lived in were a bit cramped, but he didn't want to take on the whole palaver of gardens and roofs and drains in a house. He was probably looking for something like a town house. In the old days, like every day up to this, Lena would have immediately said she would make inquiries about town houses, and go to endless trouble ringing up

zufrieden
nachgaben •
schwachsinnig •
ausgebeutet •
betrogen •
durchschaut •
abzuspülen •
eng •
Theater •
Abflüsse
Erkundigungen einziehen

Übung 36

Vervollständigen Sie die folgenden Sätze mit dem passenden Wort.
(well-briefed, wash up, current, mad, satisfied)

1. Lena knew everything about Shay's ____________ and past girlfriends.

2. Shay always went into meetings ____________ by Lena.

3. Somehow, Maggie always drove men ____________.

4. Shay's mother was never ____________.

5. Shay liked to cook but not to ____________.

auctioneers and estate agents. This time she made no offers.

'What about your house or flat, is it what you want?' he asked, almost cursorily, as if he had felt that he might have been talking just a little too much about himself.

'Oh, it's fine. I'm very happy there,' she said. She told him it was a garden flat and had plenty of light as well as nice shrubs and bushes outside big windows. He nodded briskly but seemed to look at her with slightly more interest.

On the long drive to London, they talked about friends. Shay said that he ran with a very lively crowd. No, they weren't around on weekends much, but then, he often came into the office on Saturday afternoons to do a little catching up. Lena knew this only too well. She had to cope with the results of it on Mondays: confused notes, complicated questions. She had begun every week for as long as she could remember by sorting out his thoughts for a secretary to type up. He had got all the credit. Somehow it was disappointing to know he came in only because he was bored on Saturday afternoons. She had thought it was ambition.

cursorily: nebenbei • garden flat: Wohnung mit Gartenanteil • shrubs: Sträucher • briskly: knapp • ran with a very lively crowd: einen sehr lebhaften Freundeskreis hatte • do a little catching up: ein bisschen aufzuholen • confused: verwirrt • to type up: zum Abtippen • credit: Anerkennung • ambition: Ehrgeiz

Übung 37 Sind die folgenden Aussagen wahr oder falsch?
Tragen Sie ein T für true oder ein F für false in die Kästchen ein.

1. ☐ Lena told Shay that she liked her flat.
2. ☐ Shay had no friends at all.
3. ☐ The drive to London was very short.
4. ☐ Shay worked in the office every Saturday because he was very ambitious.
5. ☐ Lena had never got any credit for sorting out Shay's thoughts for a secretary to type up.

He took his washing to his mother, it turned out. She could not believe it, but it was true. He had to go and see the woman once a week anyway, and she had a machine, so it made sense to leave her one load and collect another. And she liked it; what else had she to do?

By the time the signposts saying Central London came up, Lena had opened more doors than she might have wished to in Shay's life.

He suggested they grab something to eat, and she said thank you but no. She had friends to see in London, so unless there was anything they wanted to discuss about work for the conference tomorrow, she would leave him to his own devices.

He seemed quite put out by this. Lena looked at his handsome face scowling with almost childlike disappointment.

'Don't tell me you're going to do the clubland circuit in London?' he asked, not very kindly.

'Lord no, that's not my world at all. Just dinner with friends.'

It was true. Dinner with two old school friends – one a nun, one a nurse. They laughed and talked over old

Wegweiser

schnell eine Kleinigkeit zu essen

ihn sich selbst überlassen • verärgert • das sich böse verzog • durch die Klubs ziehen

Nonne

6. ☐ Shay's mother had too much else to do to wash her son's clothes.

7. ☐ Lena found out more negative things about Shay than she might have wished to.

8. ☐ Lena enjoyed going to clubs.

9. ☐ Shay was disappointed that Lena did not spend the evening with him.

10. ☐ Lena had dinner with two old school friends in London.

times. Something was lighter in Lena's laugh; she felt it wasn't an effort.

Next day they worked companionably at the conference, but she excused herself at lunchtime to sneak in a little shopping and said that she had a theatre date in the evening. He was thoroughly bad-tempered on the second day of the conference.

dazwischenzuschieben • ernsthaft

'Are you going to keep running away all the time, or will we see each other at all?' he grumbled.

Big blue eyes wide, she said that honestly she was sorry … but since they never went out socially at home, she assumed it would be the same here. But, of course, she would be delighted to have dinner with him if he had anywhere in mind.

'I thought you might arrange somewhere,' he said.

'Oh no, I wouldn't dream of it. If you are asking me to dinner, then you must, of course, choose where.'

träumen

It would once have been her wildest dream. Not only was the place expensive and romantic, but as he told her tale after tale of being misunderstood, betrayed, cheated, having got even, he took her hand.

'You're very easy to talk to, Lena, and you look very lovely. I hadn't realized.' She had smiled. It was a smile

betrogen • es heimgezahlt • man kann … gut mit Ihnen reden

Übung 38 Viele Ausdrücke haben eine übertragene Bedeutung, die sich nicht aus der Bedeutung der Einzelwörter ableiten lässt. Ergänzen Sie in den folgenden Ausdrücken von dieser Doppelseite die fehlenden Wörter.

1. Shay got ______________ with those who had betrayed him.
2. Shay suggested having the ______________ in Lena's room.
3. Lena had managed to ______________ Shay of any lovable quality.
4. Lena had been under Shay's ______________ all the time.
5. Being with Shay would have meant putting ______________ with his moods.

of someone who had known that this was predictable, not of someone who thought it was perfect.
When the evening ended and he suggested a brandy in his room, she said no. Perhaps she would prefer to have the nightcap in her room, he suggested, probably thinking that this was the height of sensitivity. No nightcap at all, Lena said. She who had planned this night for so long, and all it would lead to.
At one stage she began to wonder if Maggie had set her up. Every single harmless question she had asked had brought such a negative response that she had managed to strip Shay, the man she had loved for years, of any lovable quality. It was as if Maggie had known the answers in advance.

vorhersehbar
einen Schlummertrunk ... einzunehmen • Gipfel
ihr eine Falle gestellt • harmlos • Antwort • berauben • Eigenschaft

Maggie hadn't suggested that Lena talk to Shay of love.
But that night she did. They were in a restaurant looking out on the river, and he told her that he thought he loved her – yes, strange as it might seem, and having worked together for so long – but he did think he loved her.
She looked at him for a long time.
'Well, say something,' he said petulantly.
'I don't have any words,' she said truthfully.
He reached for her hands, but she pulled them away.
'What are you thinking about?' she asked him.
'How nice it is to love you, how there you were under my nose all the time.'
At least, she thought, at least he is honest in a childish sort of way. It must be nice for him to think he's found a ready-made love under his nose, as he put it.
For years she had seen how suitable she would be for him, how right as a companion, a friend, a wife. How much she would help his career and cope with his weaknesses.
Until tonight she had never seen what it would be like for her. A lifetime of putting up with his moods, build-

gereizt
vor meiner Nase
fix und fertig
zurechtzukommen mit

niedergeschlagen • ein Auge zudrücken • Blondinen ausführen

ing him up when he was low, lying for him, pretending for him. And turning a blind eye when he wanted to run with a lively crowd and do the clubs and walk the blondes.

Menge

She smiled at him affectionately. It was the way she had seen her aunt Maggie smile at a multitude of men.

schmollte • abgetan • nicht ernst genommen

'What are *you* thinking about?' he asked. He was sulking now; his declaration of love had not only not been returned, it had been smiled at, patted down, soothed away.

'I was thinking about going home, about driving out of the ferry and going home,' she said.

This was a very puzzling response. 'Why, what will you do then?' he was anxious to know.

überholen

Lena wondered what would she do. She wouldn't leave her job just because he had said he loved her and she wouldn't love him back. She liked her work, she would stay there and overtake him if necessary. She would not fight with him or explain or apologize – Maggie never did that. She was happy in her garden flat, and now she was free as well. If some man came along – as men came along for Maggie – that she really did like, then she was free to love him.

Übung 39

Bringen Sie die folgenden Aussagen in die richtige Reihenfolge und tragen Sie die entsprechenden Nummern in die Kästchen ein.

1 Lena had had a crush on her boss, Shay, for four years.
☐ When Lena excused herself at lunchtime, too, Shay became bad-tempered.
☐ Lena's aunt Maggie advised Lena to stop loving Shay because it was not healthy to love a man without being loved in return.
☐ Shay told Lena that he was in love with her.
☐ Shay asked Lena to come on a business trip to London with him.

'What will I do?' she answered him almost dreamily. The world was so full of possibilities now that the question was hard to answer. 'What will I do when I get home? I think I'll telephone my aunt.'

- [ ] Maggie told Lena that she should give up all notion of Shay if they were not seeing each other after that trip.
- [ ] Shay and Lena went to a restaurant together.
- [ ] Then Maggie sat down with Lena for three hours and gave her advice on how to make Shay love her.
- [ ] In London, Lena had dinner with two old school friends instead of going out with Shay.
- [ ] During the drive to London, Lena found out lots of negative things about Shay.
- [ ] However, Lena had noticed in the meantime that she did not love Shay anymore.

Travelling Hopefully

They were full of envy at the office when Meg told them she was going to Australia for a month on December 11. — Neid

'The weather,' they said, 'the weather.'

She would miss the cold, wet weeks in London when the streets were so crowded the traffic was at a standstill, when people were fussed and it was also so commercialized.

'Lucky Meg,' they said, and even the younger ones, the girls in their twenties, seemed genuinely jealous of her. This made Meg smile to herself.

Even though she was fifty-three, which didn't feel terribly old, she knew that most of the people she worked with thought she was well over the hill. They knew she had a grown-up son in Australia, but because they knew he was married they weren't interested in

she was … over the hill: sie hätte ihre beste Zeit hinter sich • *grown-up*: erwachsen

Übung 40

Setzen Sie die eingeklammerten Präpositionen in die richtigen Lücken ein. Achtung: Drei Präpositionen kommen doppelt vor.
(on, of, at, for, in, to, over)

1. Meg was going ________ Australia ________ a month ________ December 11.
2. Meg's colleagues were full ________ envy. They were jealous ________ her.
3. This made Meg smile ________ herself.
4. Many of Meg's colleagues thought she was ________ the hill.
5. The traffic ________ London was often ________ a standstill.

him. That, and because he didn't come back home to visit his mum. Married or single they would have been interested had they only seen her handsome Robert. Robert who had been captain of his school, who got so many A levels. Robert, aged twenty-five and married to a girl called Rosa, a Greek girl that Meg had never met.

Robert wrote and said the wedding would be quiet, but it didn't look very quiet, Meg thought, when she got the photographs. There seemed to be dozens and dozens of Greek relatives and friends. Only the groom's family was missing. She tried hard to keep her voice light when she asked him about this on the telephone. He had been impatient, as she had known he would be.

'Don't fuss, Mum,' he had said – as he had said since he was five years old and appeared with blood-soaked bandages around his knee.

'Rosa's people were all here, you and Dad would have had to come thousands of miles. It's not important. You'll come someday when we all have more time to talk.'

And of course, he had been right. A wedding where most of the cast spoke Greek, where she would have to

Primus • der die Abiturprüfung in so vielen Fächern bestanden hatte

Bräutigam

blutgetränkt

Anwesende

Übung 41 Bringen Sie die Buchstaben der unten stehenden Wörter in die richtige Reihenfolge.
Um welche Wörter aus dem Text handelt es sich?

1. falri ______
2. moorg ______
3. abddeklooo-s ______
4. trep ______
5. tasc ______
6. telunest ______
7. tainpac ______

meet Gerald, her ex-husband, and probably his pert little wife, and make conversation with them ... it would have been intolerable. Robert had been right. — *keck*

And now she was off to see them, to meet Rosa, the small dark girl in the photographs. She was going to spend a month in the sunshine, see places that she had only seen in magazine articles or on television. They would have a big party to welcome her once she had got over the jet lag. They must think she was very frail, Meg decided; they were giving her four days to recover. — *war sie auf dem Weg*; *gebrechlich*

Robert had written excitedly: they would take Meg to the Outback*, show her the real Australia. She would not be just a tourist seeing a few sights, she would get to know the place. Secretly she wished he would have said that she could sit all day in the little garden and use the neighbors' swimming pool. Meg had never known a holiday like that. For so many years there had been no holiday at all, as she saved and saved to get Robert the clothes, the bikes, and the extras that she hoped would make up for the fact that he was missing a father. Gerald had done nothing for the boy except to unsettle him about three times a year with false — *entschädigen*; *verunsichern*

info

Unter dem Begriff Outback versteht man die entweder nur dünn oder gar nicht besiedelten Gebiete abseits der Städte in Australien. Die wenigen Bewohner des Outbacks sind vor allem Farmer und Aborigines, australische Ureinwohner.

Das Outback umfasst verschiedene Landschaftsformen, darunter Steppen, Wüsten und Regenwälder.

Die berühmteste Sehenswürdigkeit des Outbacks ist vermutlich der unter dem Namen Ayers Rock bekannt gewordene Sandsteinberg, welcher von den Einheimischen Uluru genannt wird.

promises and dreams, and then gave him a battered guitar which had meant more to the boy than anything his mother had worked so hard to provide. It was while playing his guitar during his year in Australia that he had met Rosa and discovered a love and a lifestyle that were going to be forever, he told his mother.

In Meg's office they clubbed together and bought her a suitcase. It was a lovely light case, far too classy for her, she thought. Not at all the case for someone who never made a foreign journey. She could hardly believe it was crowded, they told her, this time of year all the rellies were heading down under.

'Rellies?' Meg was confused.

'People's grannies, you know,' said the young man at the desk.

Meg had wondered whether Rosa might be pregnant. But then they would never be heading for the Outback, wherever it was. She must not ask. She steeled herself over and over not to ask questions that she knew would irritate.

They settled into the plane and a big square man beside her put out his hand to introduce himself.

ramponiert • bedeutet • dafür zu sorgen
legten … zusammen
Verwandte • nach Australien fuhren • Omas
schwanger
wappnete
ließen sich … nieder • kantig • streckte … aus

Übung 42 In jeder Zeile steht ein Wort, das nicht zu den anderen passt. Streichen Sie es durch.

1. guitar – chess set – granny – suitcase

2. hand – lap – nose – spectacles

3. provide – pregnant – classy – square

4. ask – question – answer – plane

5. meet – book – remain – hand

'Since we're going to be sleeping together in a manner of speaking, I think we should know each other's names,' he said in a broad Irish accent. 'I'm Tom O'Neill from Wicklow.' — gewissermaßen

'I'm Meg Matthews from London.' She shook his hand, and hoped he wouldn't want to talk for the next twenty-four hours. She wanted to prepare her mind and practice not saying things that would make Robert say 'Don't fuss, Mum.' In fact, Tom O'Neill from Wicklow was an ideal neighbor. He had a small chess set and a book of chess problems. He perched his spectacles on his nose and went methodically through the moves. Meg's magazine and novel remained unopened on her lap. She did a mental checklist. She would *not* ask Robert what he earned a year, whether he had any intention of returning to the academic studies he had abandoned after two years of university, when he went to find himself in Australia and found singing in cafes and Rosa instead. Meg told herself over and over that she would say nothing about how infrequently he telephoned. She wasn't aware that her lips moved as she promised that she would allow no words of loneliness or criticism to escape. — Schachspiel • setzte • Brille • blieben • Schoß • verdiente • Absicht

'It's only a bit of air turbulence,' said Tom O'Neill to her reassuringly.

'I beg your pardon?' — Verzeihung? •

'I thought you were saying the Rosary. I wanted to tell you there was no need. Save it till things get really bad.' — Rosenkranz

He had a nice smile.

'No, I don't say the Rosary actually. How does it work?'

'Irregularly, I would say, like maybe one time out of fifty, but people are so pleased when it does, they think it works all the time and they forget the times it doesn't.' — unregelmäßig • einmal von fünfzig

'And do you say it?' she asked.

'Not nowadays, I did when I was a young fellow. Once it worked spectacularly. I won at the horses, the dogs, and poker. All in one week.' He looked very happy at the memory.

'I don't think you were meant to pray about those kinds of things. I didn't think it worked for gambling.'

'It didn't in the long run,' he said ruefully, and went back to his chess.

Meg noticed that Tom O'Neill drank nothing and ate little; he had glass after glass of water. Eventually she commented on it. The meals were one of the few pleasures of long-haul flying, and the drink would help sleep.

'I have to be in good shape when we arrive,' he said.

'I've read that the secret is buckets and buckets of water.'

'You're very extreme the way you take things,' Meg said to him, half admiring, half critical.

'I know,' Tom O'Neill said, 'that has been the curse and the blessing of my life.'

There were still fifteen hours to go. Meg didn't encourage any stories of his life. Not so early in the

Pferderennen • dass man um … beten sollte • Glücksspiel • auf lange Sicht • reuevoll • machte … eine Bemerkung dazu • Langstreckenfliegen • in Form • kübelweise • Fluch • Segen • ermutigen

Übung 43 Welches der angegebenen Wörter passt in die Lücke?

1. Tom had won money at the ____________.

- [ ] horses
- [ ] lions
- [ ] police station

2. Tom thought that he was not ____________ to see a wedding day.

- [ ] pointless
- [ ] modern
- [ ] likely

3. Meg thought that the meals in the plane were one of the few pleasures of ____________.

- [ ] language
- [ ] long-haul flying
- [ ] gambling

trip. When they had only four hours left she began to ask him about his life. It was a story of a daughter who had been wild. Once the girl's mother had died, Tom hadn't been able to control her. The girl had done what she liked when she liked. Now she was living in Australia. Not just staying there, mind, but living there. With a man. Not a husband, but what they called a De Facto. Very liberal, very modern, his daughter living with a man openly and telling the Australian government this too, proud as punch. He shook his head, angry and upset by it all.

man stelle sich das mal vor • Lebensgefährte • stolz wie ein Pfau

'I suppose you will have to accept it. I mean coming all this way, it would be a bit pointless if you were to attack her about it,' Meg said. It was so easy to be wise about other people's business.

She told him in turn about Robert, and how she hadn't been invited to the wedding. Tom O'Neill said wasn't it a blessing? She'd have had to make conversation to her ex and a lot of people who hadn't a word of any language between them. Much better to go now. What was a wedding day? It was only a day – not that he seemed likely to be having the opportunity of seeing one in his circumstances.

keine gemeinsame Sprache sprachen • wahrscheinlich

4. Meg didn't __________________ Tom to tell her any stories of his life.

☐ drink ☐ encourage ☐ begin

5. Praying about winning at the races didn't work for Tom __________________.

☐ in the long run ☐ mind ☐ ruefully

6. Tom was drinking buckets and buckets of water because he wanted to be __________________ when they arrived in Australia.

☐ wild ☐ tired ☐ in good shape

His daughter was called Deirdre, a good Irish name, but now she signed herself Dee, and her man friend was called Fox. What kind of name was that for a human being?

The blinds were raised. They had orange juice and hot towels to wake them up. Meg and Tim felt like old friends by this stage. They were almost loath to part. As they waited for their luggage they gave each other advice.

'Try not to mention their wedding day,' Tom warned.

'Don't say anything about the living-in-sin bit. They don't think that way here,' she begged.

'I wrote out my address,' he said.

'Thank you, thank you.' Meg felt guilty that she hadn't thought to write her son's address. Perhaps it was because she did not want Robert to think she was pathetic, picking up a strange Irishman on the plane and giving him her phone number.

'I'll leave it to you then … to get in touch or whatever,' he said, and she could sense the disappointment in his voice.

'Yes, yes, what a good idea,' Meg said.

'It's just a month is a long time,' he said.

Earlier they had both told each other that it was a very short time. Now they were on Australian soil and both of them slightly nervous of meeting their children … it seemed too long.

'It's in Randwick,' Meg began.

'No, no, you ring me if you'd like a cup of coffee someday. Maybe we could have a bit of a walk and a chat.'

He looked frightened. The endless glasses of water had left him in no state to deal with a man called Fox on equal terms. He didn't look like a man who was going to remember that his daughter called herself Dee and that she thought she *was* married, a De Facto being more or less the same. Meg felt protective of him.

Mensch • Rollos • hochgezogen • trennten sich fast ungern
In-Sünde-Leben
habe … aufgeschrieben
mitleiderregend • weil sie … aufriss • überlasse es Ihnen • spüren
Boden • etwas
mit … umzugehen • auf Augenhöhe

'Certainly I'll call you. In fact, I think we will both possibly need to escape a little from the culture shock,' she said.

auf jeden Fall

She knew she looked anxious. She could feel the frown developing on her forehead, the squeezing of her eyebrows together which made people at work say that Meg was getting into a tizz, and made her son beg her to stop fussing. She wished she could go on talking to this easy man. Why couldn't they sit down on chairs and talk for an hour or so, get themselves ready for a very different kind of Christmas than they had ever had before, and for a different lifestyle.

Zusammenziehen ihrer Augenbrauen • sich schrecklich aufregte

She realized suddenly that this was what they were both doing. They were coming to give their blessing to new lifestyles. Tom was here to tell Dee that he was glad she had found Fox and he didn't mind about their not being married properly. She was here to tell Robert that she couldn't wait to meet her new daughter-in-law and all her family, and not to hint that she ever gave her absence from their actual wedding day a thought. It would be good to meet Tom again and to know how it was all going. If they had been old friends, then obviously they would have done, but being single

anzudeuten • Abwesenheit • eigentlich

Übung 44

Was passt in die Lücken: Das eingeklammerte Adjektiv oder das zugehörige regelmäßige Adverb, welches durch Anhängen von -ly gebildet wird?

1. Robert and Meg were both ________________ (slight) nervous.
2. Meg felt ________________ (protective) of Robert.
3. She knew that she looked ________________ (anxious).
4. Meg ________________ (sudden) realised why she had come to Australia.
5. She tried to forget that she had been absent from her son's ________________ (actual) wedding day.

and middle-aged and having just met on the plane it would call for many more explanations. Possibly Robert would pity her. Or else Rosa would think that it was wonderful, perhaps, that Mother had actually found herself a bloke on a plane trip. In either case it would have been embarrassing.

erfordern • sonst

Kerl • peinlich

'I thought I might tell Deirdre, *Dee*, her name is Dee. Lord God, I must remember her name is Dee,' Tom began.

'Yes?'

'I thought I might tell her that you and I were friends from way back. You know?'

seit Langem

'I know,' she said, with a very warm smile.

They could have said more, a great deal more. In fact, they needed to find out a bit more about each other if they were meant to be friends. But it was too late. They were wheeling their trolleys through the passage to where a crowd of sun-tanned, healthy-looking young Australians waited for the crumpled rellies to stagger from the long journey. And people were calling and crying out and raising children up in the air to wave. And it seemed to be the middle of summer.

viel

zogen • sonnengebräunt

wanken

winken

Übung 45 Welche Satzteile passen zusammen?
Tragen Sie die entsprechenden Buchstaben in die Kästchen ein.

1. ☐ Meg did not want anyone to think

2. ☐ Robert wanted to tell his daughter

3. ☐ When Meg and Robert arrived in Australia,

4. ☐ Meg started to cry

5. ☐ Dee's boyfriend was called Fox

And there was Robert in shorts with long, suntanned legs and his arm around the neck of a tiny little girl with huge eyes and black curly hair biting her lip anxiously as they raked the crowd to find Meg; and when they saw her, Robert shouted, 'There she is!' as if nobody else had travelled all those hours on the plane, and they were hugging her and Rosa was crying.

'You are so young, too young to be a grandmother,' she said, and patted her little tummy with such pride that Meg started to cry too. And Robert held her and didn't ask her not to fuss. Over her son's shoulder Meg could see Tom O'Neill's beautiful daughter, the girl who had been wild all her life but didn't look wild anymore. Dee was shyly introducing a round-faced, redheaded, bespectacled boy who was loosening the unaccustomed collar and tie he had put on specially to meet the father-in-law from Ireland. Tom was indicating the boy's hair, making some joke maybe about how he knew now why he was called Fox. Whatever he said, they were all laughing.

And now Robert and Rosa were laughing too as they wiped their tears and led her toward the car. Meg

tiny: winzig
raked: absuchten
were hugging: umarmten
tummy: Bäuchlein
shyly: schüchtern •
loosening: lockerte •
unaccustomed: ungewohnt •
tie: Krawatte •
indicating: zeigte auf
wiped: wischten … ab

a) when her daughter-in-law told her that she was pregnant.

b) because he had red hair.

c) that she had found herself a bloke on a plane trip.

d) their children were already waiting for them.

e) that he and Meg were friends from way back.

zufällig • wurde gerade weggebracht

looked back in case she could catch the eye of her friend Tom O'Neill, the old friend she had met by chance on the plane. But he, too, was being bundled off. It didn't matter. They would meet here in Australia, maybe two or three times so that they would not always be in the young people's way. But not too often, because a month was a very short time for a visit. And Christmas was for families. And anyway they could always meet back on the other side of the world in a time and a place where there wouldn't be so much to do.

Lösungen

1
1. A woman whose husband has died is called a **widow**.
2. The opposite of male is **female.**
3. Janet was unhappy with her life. She was **discontented** with it.
4. Most people laugh when you **tickle** them.
5. Tony Bari did not have a beard. He had a **mustache**.
6. When someone **weeps**, he or she is usually sad.
7. In the end, Tony did not marry Miss Vogel but a lady of **property**.

2
1. Francesca asked Miss Vogel to mail a postcard from a **health spa**.
Francesca bat Fräulein Vogel, eine Postkarte aus einem Kurort abzuschicken.

2. Marion was usually not very cheerful because **she had problems with her husband**.
Marion war normalerweise nicht sehr fröhlich, da sie Schwierigkeiten mit ihrem Ehemann hatte.

3. Miss Vogel did not go to the lake with her brothers and sisters and their families because **they never asked her to come with them**.
Fräulein Vogel fuhr nicht mit ihren Geschwistern und ihren Familien zum See, da sie sie niemals fragten, ob sie mitkommen wollte.

4. When Miss Vogel went to Bloomingdale's with Heidi, they bought **clothes for the summer holidays**.
Als Fräulein Vogel mit Heidi bei Bloomingdale's war, kauften sie Kleidung für die Sommerferien.

3
1. Marion and her husband went to an inn in the **countryside**.
2. Miss Vogel liked Frank because he was a very **courteous** person.
3. Whenever Frank came to visit her, Miss Vogel gave him home-baked **shortbread**.

4
1. [F] Heather und Heidi hatten viel Zeit miteinander verbracht.
2. [F] Francesca hatte ihren beiden Liebhabern gesagt, dass sie keinen von beiden heiraten wollte.
3. [F] Tony Baris Frau hatte ihren Urlaub in Italien genossen.
4. [T] **Fräulein Vogel hatte einige Sehenswürdigkeiten in New York besichtigt.**
5. [T] **Tony Baris Frau war neidisch auf Fräulein Vogel.**
6. [T] **Tony Baris Frau schaffte es nicht, dass Fräulein Vogel aufhörte, zu lächeln.**

5
1. [e] Miss Vogel had come to the delicacies shop **because she wanted to buy food for Frank's birthday.**
Fräulein Vogel war in den Feinkostladen gekommen, da sie Essen für Franks Geburtstag kaufen wollte.

2. [a] She put the ingredients for Frank's feast **in her shopping basket.**
Sie legte die Zutaten für Franks Festmahl in ihren Einkaufskorb.

3. [c] Tony Bari had changed a lot; he was now **fat and balding.**
Tony Bari hatte sich sehr verändert; er war jetzt dick und bekam eine Glatze.

4. [b] Miss Vogel recognised that **Tony Bari would not have made her a good husband.**
Fräulein Vogel erkannte, dass Tony Bari kein guter Ehemann für sie gewesen wäre.

5. [d] People who have a lot of possessions **are not automatically happier than others.**
Leute, die viel besitzen, sind nicht automatisch glücklicher als andere.

6

b	e	r	i	f	t	e	d	y	s
l	o	s	n	o	i	l	f	w	t
g	i	v	s	o	c	b	t	t	e
a	p	p	a	l	l	i	n	g	y
v	a	u	n	i	i	a	f	s	m
e	l	m	e	s	e	f	c	o	d
r	n	d	l	h	n	o	p	e	r
a	r	t	i	o	t	b	e	l	g
g	r	e	h	e	a	r	s	e	a
e	n	y	t	h	w	d	i	t	s

7

1. Pat and Stuart lived **in** a peaceful community.
2. The adventure playground was **at** the end of the road.
3. Pat and Stuart were aware **of** their children's needs.
4. They made many sacrifices **for** their children.
5. On weekends, Pat, Stuart and their children went **to** their allotment.
6. Stuart talked **with** enthusiasm about his plan.

8

food and drink	**clothes**	**electrical appliances**
bar of chocolate	jockey shorts	circular saw
gin and lime	negligee	hairdryer
mushroom	skirt	telephone
shortbread	underwear	transistor radio

9

[1] Pat went to the hairdresser.
Pat ging zum Friseur.

[2] Pat was embarrassed by the hairdresser's questions.
Die Fragen der Friseurin waren Pat peinlich.

[3] The baby-sitter arrived on time.
Die Babysitterin kam pünktlich.

[4] Pat and Stuart said goodbye to their children.
Pat und Stuart verabschiedeten sich von ihren Kindern.

[5] Stuart suggested taking the tube.
Stuart schlug vor, die U-Bahn zu nehmen.

[6] Pat examined herself in her compact mirror.
Pat betrachtete sich prüfend in ihrem Taschenspiegel.

10

1. Pat and Stuart **walked** out of the station and towards the house where the party was going to take place.
2. Pat **asked** Stuart whether she would have to take off her clothes immediately.
3. Stuart **said** that he didn't know.
4. There **were** tears in Pat's eyes while they were talking.
5. Pat **looked** at Stuart, her eyes flashing.
6. She **begged** Stuart not to go to the wife-swapping party.
7. Stuart **tried** to put his arm around Pat, but she wouldn't let him.
8. Pat **pushed** Stuart away.
9. Stuart **could** not understand Pat. He was puzzled by her reaction.
10. He **thought** that Pat also wanted to go to the wife-swapping party.
11. Pat **was** very unhappy.
12. She **blew** her nose.

11

1. Pat feared that someone could **discover** that she and Stuart were going to a wife-swapping party.
2. She believed that women were more **sensible** about sex than men.
3. Stuart recognised how **pathetic** it might all have been.
4. In a great wave of **affection**, Pat realised how much she loved her husband.

12

hassle = **bother**
smart = **elegant**
case ~ **luggage**
tag = **label**
wrist ~ **arm**
apologetic = **sorry**

13

	Britisches Englisch	Amerikanisches Englisch	Deutsch
1.	[f] autumn	**fall**	Herbst
2.	[e] biscuit	**cookie**	Keks
3.	[g] crisps	**potato chips**	Chips
4.	[b] holiday	**vacation**	Urlaub
5.	[c] lift	**elevator**	Aufzug
6.	[a] motorway	**highway**	Autobahn
7.	[d] underground	**subway**	U-Bahn

14 **1.** When Annie opened the suitcase in the hotel, she noticed **that it was not hers**.
Als Annie im Hotel den Koffer öffnete, merkte sie, dass es nicht ihrer war.

2. Annie and Alan had picked up each other's suitcases because **both suitcases were decorated with the same initials**.
Annie und Alan hatten den Koffer des jeweils anderen mitgenommen, da beide Koffer mit denselben Initialen verziert waren.

15 **1.** [e] Alan was very angry that **he had lost his suitcase**.
Alan war sehr ärgerlich, dass er seinen Koffer verloren hatte.

2. [a] At first Annie wanted to go out to the airport, **but then she realised that she would have to wait**.
Zunächst wollte Annie zum Flughafen hinausfahren, aber dann wurde ihr bewusst, dass sie warten musste.

3. [d] The people in the hotel tried to convince Annie **that the case would be returned the following day**.
Die Leute im Hotel versuchten, Annie davon zu überzeugen, dass der Koffer am nächsten Tag zurückgegeben werden würde.

4. [b] Alan Green's address **was taped inside the lid of the case**.
Im Kofferdeckel klebte Alan Greens Adresse.

5. [c] Annie was going to go on a holiday **with her married lover**.
Annie würde mit ihrem verheirateten Geliebten in den Urlaub fahren.

16 **1.** **life raft** (Rettungsboot)
Alle anderen Wörter bezeichnen Schriftstücke.

2. **air hostess** (Stewardess)
Alle anderen Wörter bezeichnen Berufe, die an einer Schule ausgeübt werden.

3. **minibar** (Minibar)
Alle anderen Wörter bezeichnen Getränke.

4. **line** (Text)
Alle anderen Wörter bezeichnen Teile von Kleidungsstücken.

5. **creepy** (unheimlich)
Alle anderen Adjektive drücken etwas Positives aus.

6. **ring** (Läuten)
Alle anderen Wörter bezeichnen Menschen.

17 **1.** [F] Alan sah aus wie ein Fuchs, mit scharf geschnittenen Zügen und einem listigen, spitzen Gesicht.
2. [F] Annie war sich sicher, dass sie Alan noch niemals zuvor in ihrem Leben gesehen hatte.
3. [T] **Alan und Annie entschuldigten sich dafür, dass sie in den Koffer des anderen geschaut hatten.**

4. [F] Annie hatte Alans Koffer durchwühlt, um herauszufinden, was für Kleidung er am liebsten mochte.
5. [F] Alan hatte Annies Tagebuch nicht gelesen.
6. [T] **Einen Augenblick lang dachten Alan und Annie darüber nach, miteinander auszugehen.**
7. [T] **Letzten Endes beschlossen Alan und Annie, nicht miteinander auszugehen, da sie sich an die schlechten Dinge erinnerten, die sie herausgefunden hatten, als sie die geheimen Dokumente des anderen gelesen hatten.**

18
1. hour
2. to reek
3. wrong
4. burst
5. church
6. retort
7. garlic

19
storm – **to storm** – stormy
protection – to protect – **protective**
pretence – to pretend – pretended
anticipation – to anticipate – anticipatory
air – **to air** – airy

20
1. Rupert said that failing his exam was **both** a waste of money **and** a disgrace.
2. His father replied that failing an exam was **neither** a cause for alarm **nor** anything to worry about.
3. Rupert's father said that he needed **either** Rupert **or** someone else to join him in the office.
4. Rupert liked thinking **both** about the way people lived **and** their houses.
5. Rupert's parents expected their son to study **either** law **or** some other academic subject.
6. When Rupert told his parents that he was going to work as a junior in an estate agent's, his parents were **neither** pleased **nor** displeased.

21
a posh **school**
a vain **search**
a crowded **house**
a narrow **stick**
a nice **delicatessen**
a communal **coronary arrest**
a soggy **cake**

22 gay – schwul – fröhlich
pet – Liebling – Haustier
fair – ordentlich – hell
man – Mann – Mensch
reason – Vernunft – Grund
issue – Ausgabe – Angelegenheit

23
1. Jimmy had been saving with a building society for four years.
2. The estate agency had been trying to sell the cottage for a long time.
3. Rupert and Jimmy knew they were planning their future since the moment they arrived at the cottage.
4. Rupert had been happy since the day he had met Jimmy.

24
1. Rupert was afraid that Jimmy might have a fiancée.
2. Jimmy wanted to get a suitable tenant for his house.
3. Jimmy wanted to rent the second house in order to pay his mortgage.
4. After doing the two little houses up, Jimmy and Rupert decided that they would never be for sale.
5. Jimmy and Rupert grew rock plants in their garden.

25 Aus dem Wort **astounded** lassen sich unter anderem die folgenden Wörter bilden:
add, and, as, at, aunt, dead, date, do, eat, nest, net, no, not, note, nut, one, out, sad, sand, set, son, sound, sun, tea, toe, tone.

26
1. black – **white**
2. mother – **father**
3. interesting – **boring**
4. tiny – **huge**
5. light (n) – **shadow**
6. adult (n) – **child**
7. large – **small**

27

awkward	magnificent
boring	peasantry
ivy	vicarage

Es fehlen immer die Buchstaben a, g und/oder y.
Daraus kann man das Wort gay (schwul) bilden.

28
- [x] **good**
- [ ] anguished
- [x] **gay**
- [ ] remote
- [x] **reliable**
- [ ] gypsy-like
- [x] **true**

29 **1.** [c] Rupert's father planned all week **what he was going to say to his son**.
Ruperts Vater plante die ganze Woche über, was er seinem Sohn sagen würde.

2. [d] Rupert's mother was very happy to hear **that her husband had smiled at Rupert's funny descriptions**.
Ruperts Mutter war sehr froh, als sie hörte, dass ihr Mann über Ruperts witzige Beschreibungen gelächelt hatte.

3. [b] Rupert suggested to his mother **to have a bit of time off**.
Rupert schlug seiner Mutter vor, sich etwas Zeit für sich zu nehmen.

4. [e] But his mother **wanted to get value out of her son being home**.
Aber seine Mutter wollte lieber etwas davon haben, dass ihr Sohn zu Hause war.

5. [a] Rupert was appalled **at his own insensitivity**.
Rupert war entsetzt über seinen eigenen Mangel an Einfühlsamkeit.

30 **1.** Rupert's father **struggled** all afternoon.
2. Rupert's aunt always needed things for **parish sales**.
3. Rupert's father had been happy to **ramble through** the times gone by.
4. Now he **was determined** to show his son that he was interested in his job.
5. Rupert wanted his father to **rest**.
6. Judy Hickey held her head high for **two decades**.

31 **1.** bad – **good**
2. stand up – **sit down**
3. beautiful – **ugly**
4. boring – **interesting**
5. foot – **hand**
6. separated – **united**
7. boy – **girl**

32 [X] **unselfish**
[ ] loud
[X] **efficient**
[ ] self-confident
[X] **obsessive**

33 **1.** Does Shay love Lena?
We do not know; and he does not know that Lena loves him.

2. Does Lena love Shay?
Lena is convinced that she loves Shay.
Maggie believes that Lena does not really love Shay.

3. Why does Maggie tell Lena that she should stop being obsessed with Shay?
Because Lena is almost thirty years old and should rather start a real relationship with a man.

4. Why does Lena protest that she is happy with her life?
Because she has not settled for second best, like many others.
Because she loves every second of her working day.
Because she is appreciated in her office.

34
- [X] **She has shiny, well-cut hair.**
- [ ] Her eyes are a dark brown.
- [ ] She is slim but not tall.
- [X] **She knows how to make the most of her fair complexion.**
- [ ] She can get every man she wants.
- [X] **Her thirtieth birthday is coming up.**
- [ ] Her favourite foods are wild mushrooms, brown bread and strawberries.

35

1					B	**L**	U	S	H	E	R			
2					N	**E**	P	H	E	W				
3			L	A	U	**N**	D	E	R	E	T	T	E	
4						**A**	P	P	L	Y				
						&								
5					I	**M**	P	A	T	I	E	N	C	E
6		R	E	S	E	**A**	R	C	H					
7				A	N	**G**	E	L						
8	S	T	R	I	N	**G**								
9					N	**I**	I	E	C	E				
10		B	O	T	H	**E**	R							

36
1. Lena knew everything about Shay's **current** and past girlfriends.
2. Shay always went into meetings **well-briefed** by Lena.
3. Somehow, Maggie always drove men **mad**.
4. Shay's mother was never **satisfied**.
5. Shay liked to cook but not to **wash up**.

37
1. [T] **Lena erzählte Shay, dass sie ihre Wohnung mochte.**
2. [F] Shay hatte überhaupt keine Freunde.
3. [F] Die Fahrt nach London war sehr kurz.
4. [F] Shay arbeitete jeden Samstag im Büro, weil er sehr ehrgeizig war.
5. [T] **Lena hatte nie Anerkennung dafür bekommen, dass sie Shays Gedanken ordnete, sodass eine Sekretärin sie abtippen konnte.**
6. [F] Shays Mutter war zu beschäftigt, um die Kleidung ihres Sohnes zu waschen.
7. [T] **Lena fand mehr Negatives über Shay heraus, als sie sich gewünscht hätte.**
8. [F] Lena ging gerne in Klubs.
9. [T] **Shay war enttäuscht darüber, dass Lena nicht den Abend mit ihm verbrachte.**
10. [T] **Lena hat mit zwei alten Schulfreundinnen in London zu Abend gegessen.**

38 **1.** Shay got **even** with those who had betrayed him.
2. Shay suggested having the **nightcap** in Lena's room.
3. Lena had managed to **strip** Shay of any lovable quality.
4. Lena had been under Shay's **nose** all the time.
5. Being with Shay would have meant putting **up** with his moods.

39 [1] Lena had had a crush on her boss, Shay, for four years.
Lena hatte seit vier Jahren für ihren Chef Shay geschwärmt.

[2] Lena's aunt Maggie advised her to stop loving Shay because it was not healthy to love a man without being loved in return.
Lenas Tante Maggie riet ihr, damit aufzuhören, Shay zu lieben, da es nicht gesund sei, einen Mann zu lieben, ohne zurückgeliebt zu werden.

[3] Shay asked Lena to come on a business trip to London with him.
Shay bat Lena, mit ihm auf Geschäftsreise nach London zu fahren.

[4] Maggie told Lena that she should give up all notion of Shay if they were not seeing each other after that trip.
Maggie sagte zu Lena, dass sie sich Shay aus dem Kopf schlagen sollte, falls sie nach dieser Reise kein Paar seien.

[5] Then Maggie sat down with Lena for three hours and gave her advice on how to make Shay love her.
Dann setzte sich Maggie drei Stunden lang mit Lena hin und gab ihr Ratschläge, wie sie Shay dazu bringen konnte, sie zu lieben.

[6] During the drive to London, Lena found out lots of negative things about Shay.
Während der Fahrt nach London fand Lena viel Negatives über Shay heraus.

[7] In London, Lena had dinner with two old school friends instead of going out with Shay.
In London aß Lena mit zwei alten Schulfreundinnen zu Abend, anstatt mit Shay auszugehen.

[8] When Lena excused herself at lunchtime, too, Shay became bad-tempered.
Als Lena sich auch in der Mittagspause entschuldigte, wurde Shay langsam ärgerlich.

[9] Shay and Lena went to a restaurant together.
Shay und Lena gingen gemeinsam in ein Restaurant.

[10] Shay told Lena that he was in love with her.
Shay sagte zu Lena, dass er sie liebe.

[11] However, Lena had noticed in the meantime that she did not love Shay anymore.
Lena hatte jedoch in der Zwischenzeit gemerkt, dass sie Shay nicht mehr liebte.

40
1. Meg was going **to** Australia **for** a month **on** December 11.
2. Meg's colleagues were full **of** envy. They were jealous **of** her.
3. This made Meg smile **to** herself.
4. Many of Meg's colleagues thought she was **over** the hill.
5. The traffic **in** London was often **at** a standstill.

41
1. **frail**
2. **groom**
3. **blood-soaked**
4. **pert**
5. **cast**
6. **unsettle**
7. **captain**

42
1. guitar – chess set – **granny** – suitcase
Alle anderen Wörter bezeichnen Gegenstände.

2. hand – lap – nose – **spectacles**
Alle anderen Wörter bezeichnen Körperteile.

3. **provide** – pregnant – classy – square
Alle anderen Wörter sind Adjektive.

4. ask – question – answer – **plane**
Alle anderen Wörter haben mit dem Fragenstellen zu tun.

5. meet – book – **remain** – hand
Alle anderen Wörter haben genau vier Buchstaben.

43
1. Tom had won money at the **horses**.
2. Tom thought that he was not **likely** to see a wedding day.
3. Meg thought that the meals in the plane were one of the few pleasures of **long-haul flying**.
4. Meg didn't **encourage** Tom to tell her any stories of his life.
5. Praying about winning at the races didn't work for Tom **in the long run**.
6. Tom was drinking buckets and buckets of water because he wanted to be **in good shape** when they arrived in Australia.

44
1. Robert and Meg were both **slightly** nervous.
(Das Adverb bestimmt das Adjektiv „nervous" genauer.)

2. Meg felt **protective** of Robert. (Bei Verben des Fühlens steht die Adjektivform.)

3. She knew that she looked **anxious**.
(Bei Verben der Wahrnehmung steht die Adjektivform.)

4. Meg **suddenly** realised why she had come to Australia.
(„Normale" Verben werden durch Adverbien genauer bestimmt.)

5. She tried to forget that she had been absent from her son's **actual** wedding day.
(Das Adjektiv bestimmt das Substantiv **wedding day** genauer.)

45 **1.** [c] Meg did not want anyone to think **that she had found herself a bloke on a plane trip.**
Meg wollte nicht, dass irgendjemand dachte, sie hätte sich im Flugzeug einen Mann geangelt.

2. [e] Robert wanted to tell his daughter **that he and Meg were friends from way back.**
Robert wollte seiner Tochter erzählen, dass er und Meg schon seit langem befreundet seien.

3. [d] When Meg and Robert arrived in Australia, **their children were already waiting for them.**
Als Meg und Robert in Australien ankamen, warteten ihre Kinder bereits auf sie.

4. [a] Meg started to cry **when her daughter-in-law told her that she was pregnant.**
Meg fing an zu weinen, als ihre Schwiegertochter ihr sagte, dass sie schwanger sei.

5. [b] Dee's boyfriend was called Fox **because he had red hair.**
Dees Freund hieß mit Spitznamen Fuchs, da er rote Haare hatte.

Wörterverzeichnis

A

to abandon aufgeben
about: to be (was/were – been) about im Begriff sein
absence Abwesenheit
abuse Schmähung
actual eigentlich, tatsächlich
adamant unnachgiebig
to adapt zurechtkommen
to add vergrößern
to administer vermitteln
admiration Bewunderung
adventure playground Abenteuerspielplatz
affection Zuneigung
to afford something sich etwas leisten
agency Agentur
aggrieved bedrückt
aging process Älterwerden
agreeable freundlich
ahead of vor
air hostess Stewardess
to air lüften
A levels Abiturprüfungen
allotment Schrebergarten
to allow oneself the indulgence of doing something sich etwas gönnen
ally Verbündete(r)
alpine Gebirgspflanze
ambition Ehrgeiz
angel Engel
anguished gequält
annoyed verärgert
anticipation Vorfreude
anxiety Unruhe
any old how irgendwie
anyway sowieso
apologetic zerknirscht
appalled entsetzt
appalling entsetzlich
to apply auftragen
appointment Termin
to appreciate schätzen
apprenticed: to be (was/were – been) apprenticed als Lehrling beginnen
to approach something etwas nahe kommen
appropriate angemessen
artistic künstlerisch
arty farty auf Künstler machend
as much as anything am meisten
to ask somebody out jemanden um ein Rendezvous bitten
to assume annehmen
assurance Zusicherung
astounded erstaunt
A to Z Stadtplan
attendance Besucher, Besucherzahl
attendant letter Begleitschreiben
attraction Anziehung
auctioneering business Auktionshaus
average Durchschnitt
awkward unwohl

B

background Hintergrund
bad-tempered übellaunig
balding: to be (was/were – been) balding kahl werden
to balls up vermasseln
bank clerk Bankangestellter

bar of chocolate Schokoriegel
barbed wire Stacheldraht
barely kaum
battered ramponiert
brooding: to be (was/were – been) brooding brüten
to bear (bore – borne) ertragen
beau Schatz
beauty parlor Schönheitssalon
to beg mit flehender Stimme fragen
belt Gürtel
beside neben
to bet wetten
better: she had better tell him sie sollte es ihm besser sagen
betrayed betrogen
blessing Segen
blind Rollo
bloke Kerl
blood-soaked blutgetränkt
bloody verdammt
Bloomingdale's ein Kaufhaus in New York
to blow (blew – blown) one's nose sich schnäuzen
blusher Rouge
bondage Fesselspiele
bordering on something an der Grenze zu etwas
to bore langweilen
bosom Brust
to bother sich bemühen
to bottle einmachen
boulder of rock Felsbrocken
bouquet Strauß
box number Chiffrenummer
to brace oneself sich zusammenreißen
to brand brandmarken
brave mutig
breastbone Brustbein
to brew kochen (Kaffee)
briefcase Aktenkoffer
bright wach
to brighten up verschönern
to bring (brought – brought) somebody up jemanden erziehen
briskly knapp
to brush aside beiseitewischen
buckets and buckets kübelweise
building society Bausparkasse
to bundle hineinstopfen
bundled off: to be (was/were – been) bundled off weggebracht werden
to burst (burst – burst) sich rasend ausbreiten
to burst at the seams aus allen Nähten platzen
buttoned up zugeknöpft
to button-hole löchern
by chance zufällig

C

cabbage Kohlkopf
to call for erfordern
to call in vorbeischauen
to call something off etwas abblasen
calorie-packed kalorienreich
camp tuntig
captain Primus
caravan Wohnwagen
carbonade Rostbraten
carefree unbekümmert

carousel Gepäckband
case Koffer
cast Anwesende
casual beiläufig
cautiously vorsichtig
ceaseless endlos
to celebrate feiern
to cement festigen
certainly auf jeden Fall
certifiably völlig
chalet Ferienhaus
to change gear den Gang wechseln
charm Charme
chat Schwätzchen
to cheat somebody jemanden betrügen
cheek Wange
to cheer somebody up jemanden aufmuntern
cheerful fröhlich
cheery vergnügt
chemist Apotheke
chess set Schachspiel
china Porzellan
circular saw Kreissäge
circumstance Umstand
to claim behaupten
classy fein
to clear out ausräumen
clematis Klematis
clerical work Büroarbeit
client Kunde
cling-film Frischhaltefolie
closet Schrank
to club together zusammenlegen
to coincide sich zufällig treffen
collar Kragen
to come (came – come) up näher rücken
to comment on something eine Bemerkung zu etwas machen
commission Provision
communal kollektiv
community Gemeinschaft
commuting Pendeln
compact mirror Taschenspiegel
companionably kameradschaftlich
complexion Teint
concealed versteckt
confidence Vertrauen
confidently selbstsicher
to confirm bestätigen
confused verwirrt
confusion Verlegenheit
conniving durchtrieben, hinterhältig
to consider auf die Idee kommen
to consider somebody reliable jemanden kreditwürdig befinden
conspiracy Verschwörung
contented zufrieden
conveyancing Eigentumsübertragung
conveyor belt Transportband
cooped up eingepfercht
to cope with something mit etwas fertig werden
coronary arrest Herzinfarkt
cottage Häuschen
countryside Land
courage Mut
courteous höflich
courting: to be (was/were – been) courting miteinander gehen
coyly vorsichtig

cramped eng, schwer lesbar
to crawl kriechen
crease Falte
credit Anerkennung
creeper Kletterpflanze
creepy unheimlich
to cross something etwas durchqueren
crowded überfüllt
to cruise somebody jemanden aufreißen
to crumple verschrumpeln
crush Schwärmerei
to cry rufen
cuff Manschette
to cup something in one's hands etwas mit den Händen umfassen
curled up zusammengerollt
curly lockig
current gegenwärtig
curse Fluch
cursorily nebenbei
customary einer Person eigen
Customs man Zollbeamter
cut out for something für etwas geschaffen
to cut (cut – cut) through vorbeugen

D

daily Tageszeitung
daring gewagt
dark dunkelhaarig
to dash over rübersausen
De Facto Lebensgefährte
dead-end ohne Aufstiegschancen
to deal (dealt – dealt) with somebody mit jemandem umgehen
decade Jahrzehnt
deceiving trügerisch
definite unerbittlich
degree Hochschulabschluss
to deliberate nachdenken
delicatessen Feinkostladen
delightful herrlich
to deliver liefern
department Abteilung
department store Kaufhaus
departure Abflug
descendant Nachkomme
to deserve verdienen
desire Verlangen
desperately verzweifelt
to destroy zerstören
determined fest entschlossen
developed print Abzug
devil Teufel
diary Tagebuch
dim dämmerig
disarrayed unordentlich
discontented unglücklich
to discover entdecken
disgrace Schande
to dismiss abtun
to dissolve in laughter in Gelächter ausbrechen
distressed beunruhigt
to disturb stören
to divide trennen
to do (did – done) reichen
to do a little catching up ein bisschen aufholen
to do something for a living etwas beruflich machen
to do something up etwas herrichten

to do the clubland circuit durch die Klubs ziehen
down to it konzentriert
dozen Dutzend
to drain something etwas leeren
drain Abfluss
drape Vorhang
to dream (dreamt – dreamt) träumen
to drive (drove – driven) somebody mad jemanden verrückt machen
drive Einfahrt
dry cleaner Reinigung
due: to be (was/were – been) due something etwas verdienen
dwarfed überragt
dwelling Wohnhaus

E

eager erwartungsvoll
to earn verdienen
earth-shaking weltbewegend
easily bequem
easy to talk to: to be (was/were – been) easy to talk to jemand sein, mit dem man gut reden kann
elderly älter
else sonst
embarrassing peinlich
embrace Umarmung
to encourage ermutigen
endearment Kosewort
enterprise Unternehmen
to enthuse sich begeistern
entire ganz
envious neidisch
envy Neid
to escape entfahren
essential unbedingt erforderlich
to establish a bond das Eis brechen
estate agent's Immobilienagentur
evergreen immergrüne Pflanze
examination Prüfung
to examine begutachten
executive class Business Class
exercise book Schulheft
exhausted erschöpft
to experience erleben
extra Zuschlag

F

fabulous birds tolle Frauen
faint ohnmächtig
fair hell, ordentlich
fair-haired blond
fake tan Selbstbräuner
to fall (fell – fallen) out sich aushängen
familiar bekannt
fanciful: to be (was/were – been) fanciful übertreiben
to fancy somebody auf jemanden stehen
far out weit draußen
fashionable schick
feast Festmahl
feeble schwach
to feel (felt – felt) a sense of exclusion sich ausgeschlossen fühlen
to feel like something auf etwas Lust haben
fees Schulgebühren
fellow Kerl
felt pen Filzstift
female weiblich
fervently energisch

fiancée Verlobte
fiercely äußerst
to fight (fought – fought) streiten
file Akte
filthy dreckig
finery feine Kleidung
fire Begeisterung
to fire entfachen
firmly bestimmt
First Law erstes Juraexamen
to fit in dazwischennehmen
to fix up reparieren
to flash blitzen
to flash by vorüberrasen
flashy-looking knallig
flat schal
flattering schmeichelhaft
flowery blumig
fluffy flauschig
flush Hochgefühl
to fly (flew – flown) by wie im Flug vergehen
folk Leute
fond: to be (was/were – been) fond of somebody jemanden gern haben
foolish lächerlich
for a change zur Abwechslung
for heaven's sake um Himmels willen
for sale zu verkaufen
for the rest of his/her days bis an sein/ihr Lebensende
for want of mangels
forbidden verboten
forehead Stirn
to forgive (forgave – forgiven) vergeben
to forgo (forwent – forgone) verzichten
fortune Vermögen
foul abstoßend
founder Gründer
fox Fuchs
frail gebrechlich
fraught with meaning bedeutungsschwanger
freedom Freiheit
freezer Tiefkühlfach
frequent traveller Vielflieger
from way back seit Langem
frontier Grenze
frown Stirnrunzeln
function Veranstaltung
funeral Beerdigung
fuss Hektik

G

gain Profit
gambling Glücksspiel
games Sport
garden flat Wohnung mit Gartenanteil
garment Kleidung(sstück)
gate lodge Pförtnerhäuschen
gay schwul
generosity Großzügigkeit
genius Meister
gentian Enzian
gentle sanft
gentleman's privilege Ehrensache
genuine echt
geography mistress Erdkundelehrerin
to get (got – got) a minor start ein wenig zusammenzucken

to get even with somebody es jemandem heimzahlen
to get good notice etwas frühzeitig erfahren
to get in touch Kontakt aufnehmen
to get into a tizz sich schrecklich aufregen
to get on with somebody sich mit jemandem verstehen
to get round to something: I must get round to it. Das muss ich irgendwann machen.
to get something out of one's system etwas streichen können
to get value out of something etwas von etwas haben
giant riesig
gin and lime Gin Lemon
to give (gave – given) a jump hüpfen
to give away verraten
to give a snort schnauben
to give chapter and verse genau belegen
to give in nachgeben
to give somebody directions jemandem den Weg erklären
to give up all notion of something sich etwas aus dem Kopf schlagen
glad froh
glance Blick
glasses Brille
gleam Glanz
gloomy trübsinnig
glowing überschwänglich
glumly finster
to go (went – gone) ahead weitermachen
to go along with something sich mit etwas vertragen
to go astray verloren gehen
to go by something nach etwas urteilen
to go wild durchdrehen
God Almighty! Großer Gott!
God damn and blast it! Verdammt!
God rot… zur Hölle mit …
goo schmieriges Zeug
good lieb
good-natured freundlich
gossip-column chat Klatsch
to grab something to eat schnell eine Kleinigkeit essen
granny Oma
gratitude Dankbarkeit
great: a great deal viel
greed Gier
groom Bräutigam
to grope around suchen
to grow (grew – grown) anbauen
to grow up aufwachsen
grown-up erwachsen
grubby schmuddelig
to grumble schimpfen
grumpy mürrisch
guardian angel Schutzengel
guilt Schuldgefühl
guy Kerl
gym Fitnessstudio
gypsy-like zigeunerhaft

H

to hail herbeiwinken
hairdresser Friseur
hall Diele
handy praktisch

to harbour hegen
hard-to-decipher schwer entzifferbar
harlot Hure
harmless harmlos
harsh hart
hassle Hektik
to have (had – had) a loan of mieten
to have designs on somebody es auf jemanden abgesehen haben
to have none of it nichts davon hören wollen
to have people in Besuch haben
to have pretences arranged for somebody jemandem etwas vorspielen
to have the heart to do something etwas übers Herz bringen
to have the nightcap einen Schlummertrunk einnehmen
to have time off sich frei nehmen
to head down under nach Australien fahren
head Spitze
heading Stichpunkt
headmaster Schuldirektor
heady berauscht
health food shop Reformhaus
health spa Kur
hearth rug Kaminteppich
heavy drinker starker Trinker
heavy with voller
heel Absatz
height Gipfel
hen Huhn
herb pillow Kräuterkissen
herby würzig
hesitantly zögerlich
to hide (hid – hidden) sich verstecken
to hinge on something von etwas abhängen
to hint andeuten
to hold (held – held) aufhalten
homemaker Hausfrau
homesickness Heimweh
horses: the horses Pferderennen
to hover herumstehen
huffily eingeschnappt
to hug umarmen
huge riesig
human being Mensch
to hunt herumwühlen
hunting: the huntin' shootin' fishin' set die bessere Gesellschaft

I

I beg your pardon? Verzeihung?
illicit verboten
imagination Fantasie
immaculate makellos
impatience Ungeduld
to imperil gefährden
impressed beeindruckt
in a manner of speaking gewissermaßen
in a very poor light in sehr schlechtem Licht
in: to be (was/were – been) in ankommen
in blocks en bloc
Incorporated Law Society Juristenvereinigung
in demand begehrt

in good shape in Form
in-laws Schwiegerleute
in longhand ausführlich
in return zurück
in the long run auf lange Sicht
indeed tatsächlich
to indicate something auf etwas zeigen
indication Andeutung
infatuation Schwärmerei
ingredient Zutat
ink-covered voller Tintenflecken
inn Gasthof
innocent unschuldig
insane verrückt
insensitivity Mangel an Einfühlsamkeit
to inspire awe Ehrfurcht erregen
insubstantial nicht sättigend
to intend beabsichtigen
intention Absicht
interior decorator Innenausstatter
to intrude sich aufdrängen
to invent erfinden
involved beteiligt
irregularly unregelmäßig
issue Ausgabe
ivy Efeu

J

janitor Hausmeister
jealous eifersüchtig
jockey-shorts eine Art von Unterhose
junior: position as a junior Juniorstelle

K

kebab Döner
to keep (kept – kept) einhalten
to keep an eye on somebody auf jemanden aufpassen
to keep in touch in Kontakt bleiben
to keep something going etwas am Laufen halten
kennels Hundepension

L

lace Spitze
to lack fehlen
lap Schoß
to launch into something etwas beginnen
launderette Waschsalon
to lay (laid – laid) out zurechtlegen
layer Lage
leasehold Pacht
to leave (left – left) it to somebody es jemandem überlassen
to leave somebody to his/her own devices jemanden sich selbst überlassen
lecture Vorlesung
lest damit nicht
levelly ruhig
lid Deckel
life raft Rettungsboot
likely wahrscheinlich
limp-wristed schwul
lines Text
to listen to reason Vernunft annehmen
living-in-sin In-Sünde-Leben
load Belastung, Haufen, Ladung

loaf Laib Brot
loath to part: to be (was/were – been) loath to part sich ungern trennen
long: to be long lange brauchen
long-haul flying Langstreckenfliegen
to look after somebody/something sich um jemanden/etwas kümmern
loosely: what had been loosely called sogenannt
to loosen lockern
lot Clique
lousy furchtbar
low niedergeschlagen, schummrig
ludicrous absurd
lurch Ruck

M

machinery Prozedere
magnificent wundervoll
to mail aufgeben
mainly die meisten
to maintain aufrecht erhalten
to make (made – made) a convincing case ein überzeugendes Bild ergeben
to make a public fool of oneself sich öffentlich zum Narren machen
to make free herummachen
to make inquiries Erkundigungen einziehen
to make it es schaffen
to make somebody gasp jemandem den Atem stocken lassen
to make something sound etwas sanieren
to make up for something für etwas entschädigen
make-or-break entscheidend
male männlich
mane Mähne
manor house Herrenhaus
manual Handbuch
to mark benoten
to mate sich begatten
Matins Frühgottesdienst
matter of factly sachlich
to mean (meant – meant) something to somebody jemandem etwas bedeuten
to mean to do something etwas vorhaben
mean hinterhältig
meant: to be meant to do something etwas tun sollen
meek lammfromm
merely nur
to merit verdienen
Mickey Mouse effort lachhafter Versuch
might as well kann ebenso gut
mildly sanft
mind man stelle sich das mal vor
mistress Liebhaberin
mockery Spott
money-swallowing kostspielig
Morocco Marokko
moronic schwachsinnig
morrow der nächste Tag
mortgage Hypothek
motoring holiday Urlaub mit dem Auto
motorway Autobahn

to move in with somebody mit jemandem zusammenziehen
multitude Menge
murky undurchsichtig
mustache Schnurrbart
mystified überrascht

N

narrow dünn
nausea Übelkeit
neglected vernachlässigt
negotiation Verhandlung
nephew Neffe
niece Nichte
niggling nagend
nightie Nachthemd
nightmare Albtraum
no harm: to be (was/were – been) no harm nicht schaden
no matter egal
no use: to be (was/were – been) no use nichts bringen
to nod at somebody jemandem zunicken
not give a damn about something sich nicht um etwas scheren
not have a word of any language between each other keine gemeinsame Sprache sprechen
not have an inkling nicht die leiseste Ahnung haben
nothing you could put your finger on nichts, was man genau feststellen könnte
to notice bemerken
now and then ab und zu
nuclear fall-out radioaktiver Niederschlag
nun Nonne
nursing Pflege
nutty verrückt

O

obsessed besessen
obsession fixe Idee
odd seltsam
of property wohlhabend
of the sort dergleichen
off: to be (was/were – been) off auf dem Weg sein
to offer condolences Beileid aussprechen
office Büro
on: to be (was/were – been) on drin sein
on equal terms auf Augenhöhe
on time pünktlich
one time out of fifty einmal unter fünfzig
to opt out sich drücken
orgy Orgie
ornament Verzierung
out of place fehl am Platz
outhouse Nebengebäude
outing Ausflug
out-of-the-way spot abgelegener Ort
outraged empört
hill: to be (was/were – been) over the hill die beste Zeit hinter sich haben
overgrown überwuchert
overheads Unkosten
overseas ausländisch
to overtake (overtook – overtaken) überholen

P

palaver Theater
pale blass
panel Scheibe
panicky nervös
parish sale Kirchenbasar
parochial spießig
passionate leidenschaftlich
to pat tätscheln
to pat something down etwas abtun
to patch up kitten
pathetic jämmerlich, mitleid-erregend
patio Veranda
peasantry Bauern
to perch something on something etwas auf etwas setzen
to persuade überzeugen
persuasive überzeugend
pert keck
pet Liebling
petulantly gereizt
to pick auswählen
to pick somebody up jemanden aufreißen
pickup place Abholort
piety Frömmigkeit
pile Stapel
to pin somebody to something jemanden auf etwas festnageln
to pin something to something etwas an etwas heften
pitch Stand
pity Mitleid
plan of campaign Schlachtplan
to play the heavy aunt als Tante ein Machtwort sprechen
play Theaterstück
plea Bitte
to plead bittend sagen
to please somebody es jemandem recht machen
pleasure Lust
to plot intrigieren
point Sinn
to point out zeigen
pointed spitz
to polish polieren
pool Teppich
the Pope der Papst
porch Vordach
porous porös
porter Portier
posh vornehm
positively wirklich
possession Besitz
possessive besitzergreifend
posture Haltung
to pour vinegar onto something etwas verderben
praise Lob
to pray about something um etwas beten
preachy moralisierend
precious wertvoll
predictable vorhersehbar
pregnant schwanger
to preserve einlegen
pretence Heuchelei
to pretend so tun als ob
to prevent somebody from something jemanden von etwas abhalten
pride Stolz
prissy brav

proof Beweis
to propose marriage einen Heiratsantrag machen
to proposition somebody jemanden anmachen
protective fürsorglich
proud as punch stolz wie ein Pfau
to provide something für etwas sorgen
punctual pünktlich
punishment Strafe
to push the trolley den Einkaufswagen schieben
put out verärgert
to put (put – put) out one's hand seine Hand ausstrecken
to put somebody off jemanden abwehren
to put up with something mit etwas zurechtkommen
to puzzle grübeln
puzzled verwirrt

Q

quality Eigenschaft
queue Warteschlange

R

rabidly rasend
to rail schimpfen
raised hochgezogen
raised: to be (was/were – been) raised aufwachsen
to rake absuchen
to ramble through something durch etwas streifen
ramp Rampe
rat Mistkerl
rate Tarif
raving lunatic: to be (was/were – been) a raving lunatic völlig verrückt sein
to read … auf den Namen …
to read (read – read) for a degree studieren
ready-made fix und fertig
to reassure beruhigen
rector Pfarrer
to reek stinken
regular regelmäßig
to rehearse üben
rejected gemieden
relationship Beziehung
relieved erleichtert
rellies Verwandte
to remain bleiben
remote distanziert
remotely entfernt
to remove entfernen
to rend (rent – rent) spalten
to replace ersetzen
to re-route umlenken
research Suche
resident Bewohner
resignedly ergeben
to resolve beschließen
response Antwort
to rest sich ausruhen
to retort erwidern
to reveal enthüllen
ridiculous lächerlich
riff-raff Gesindel
to right-turn rechts abbiegen
ring Läuten
to rip apart aufschlitzen

to rip somebody off jemanden ausbeuten
rockery Steingarten
rock plant Steinpflanze
roof Dach
Rosary Rosenkranz
row Streit
ruefully reuevoll
to run (ran – run) something etwas betreiben
to run with a very lively crowd einen sehr lebhaften Freundeskreis haben
to run schießen
runner bean Stangenbohne
to rush brausen
rut Trott
ruthless unbarmherzig

S

sacrifice Opfer
safe and sound wohlbehalten
sameness Eintönigkeit
satisfactory zufriedenstellend
satisfied zufrieden
schedule Zeitplan
scheming hinterhältig
School Principal Schuldirektor
to scoop up zusammenkratzen
to scowl böse das Gesicht verziehen
to scream schreien
to screw vögeln
second zweite Wahl
secret geheim
to seduce verführen
to see (saw – seen) für etwas sorgen
to see somebody jemanden treffen
to see somebody coming jemanden durchschauen
see-if-I-care gleichgültig
to seek (sought – sought) suchen
to seize einziehen
selfish egoistisch
self-sufficiency Autarkie
to send (sent – sent) for something sich etwas bringen lassen
to sense spüren
sensible vernünftig
service Gottesdienst
set in lines faltig
to set (set – set) somebody up jemandem eine Falle stellen
to set something up etwas ausmachen
to settle sich niederlassen, sich gewöhnen
to settle down sich regeln
to settle for second best sich mit dem Zweitbesten zufriedengeben
settled gestanden
shadow Schatten
shallow oberflächlich
shaming peinlich
sharp-featured mit scharfen Gesichtszügen
shelter Schutz
shiny glänzend
shopping basket Einkaufskorb
short: to be (was/were – been) short kurz angebunden sein
shortbread Buttergebäck
to show vorweisen
showy scholar Vorzeigestudent(in)
shrilly mit schriller Stimme
shrub Strauch

to shrug mit den Schultern zucken
to shudder schaudern
shuffle around the floor Tänzchen
shyly schüchtern
sigh Seufzer
signpost Wegweiser
silently still
silly dumm
sinister unheilvoll
sink Spülbecken
site Grundstück
skull Totenschädel
slap-happy locker
slicing In-Scheiben-Schneiden
slight schlank
slightly etwas
slimline kalorienreduziert
to slobber over somebody jemanden anmachen
smart schick
smoked salmon Räucherlachs
to sneak in dazwischenschieben
sneaky hinterhältig
sociability Geselligkeit
social plan Freizeitunternehmung
soda Limo
soggy matschig
soil Boden
solicitor Anwalt
somehow irgendwie
to soothe something away etwas nicht ernst nehmen
soothingly besänftigend
sophisticated kultiviert
sordid schäbig
sorrow Anteilnahme
sorry traurig
to sort out klären
soul Seele
to sow (sowed – sown) wild oats sich die Hörner abstoßen
Special Branch man Sicherheitsbeamter
specifically ausdrücklich
spectacles Brille
spicy scharf
spiritedly lebhaft
sponge bag Kulturbeutel
sponge Schwamm
to spread (spread – spread) something out etwas ausbreiten
spring Frühling
square kantig
squeezing together of one's eyebrows Zusammenziehen der Augenbrauen
staff Lehrkraft
stage direction Regieanweisung
to stagger wanken
to stammer stammeln
stark naked splitternackt
startled verblüfft
to starve verhungern
to steel onself sich wappnen
to step down absteigen
to stock lagern
stock exchange Börse
stodgy schwer verdaulich
to storm toben
to stow something etwas verstauen
strapping drall
strawberry Erdbeere
to stretch sich strecken
strictly ganz
string Reihe

to strip somebody of something jemanden einer Sache berauben
to struggle sich abmühen
to stuff passen
to succeed Erfolg haben
succinctly kurz angebunden
suddenly plötzlich
suggestive anzüglich
suitable geeignet
to sulk schmollen
sunset Sonnenuntergang
sun-tanned sonnengebräunt
superhuman übermenschlich
superintendent Hausverwalter
supply Lieferung
supportively ermutigend
supreme Führungskraft
sure I thought… ich dachte schon …
surge Welle
surprise Überraschung
survival Überleben
to suspect vermuten
suspicious argwöhnisch
to swallow schlucken
sympathetic mitfühlend

T

tag Anhänger
to taint verderben
to take (took – taken) over sich breit machen
to take somebody off mit jemandem fortfahren
to take to one's bed bettlägerig werden
to take to something etwas mögen
tale Erzählung
tame harmlos
to tape kleben
tatty abgenutzt
TD Abgeordneter
tear Träne
to tear (tore – torn) zerreißen
tedious ermüdend
telephone directory Telefonbuch
temporary vorübergehend
tenant Mieter
tension Spannung
tentatively zögernd
Thanksgiving Erntedank
to thaw auftauen
thoroughly ernsthaft
threat Drohung
threatened angedroht
to throw (threw – thrown) up something etwas hinschmeißen
to tickle kitzeln
tie Krawatte
tied up beschäftigt
tingle Prickeln
tinted getönt
tiny winzig
tissue Taschentuch
tissue paper Papiertaschentuch
toddler Kleinkind
toilet bag Kulturbeutel
transplanting Umpflanzen
treacherous treulos
to tremble zittern
trifle eine Art Nachtisch
Trinity Universität in Dublin
to trouble belästigen
true treu
to trundle off davonrollen
trunk call Ferngespräch

tube U-Bahn
tummy Bäuchlein
to turn a blind eye ein Auge zudrücken
to turn out verlaufen
to turn up auftauchen
to tut-tut „na, na“ sagen
twined verknüpft
to type tippen
to type up abtippen

U

ugly hässlich
unaccustomed ungewohnt
unconverted originalbelassen
undemanding anspruchslos
underground U-Bahn
under somebody's nose vor jemandes Nase
underlining Unterstreichung
unease Kummer
uninhibited hemmungslos
united einig
unmentionable unaussprechlich
unscathed unversehrt
unselfishly selbstlos
to unsettle verunsichern
urge Drang
to usher somebody in jemanden hineinführen
utterly: to be (was/were – been) utterly set on doing something wild entschlossen sein, etwas zu tun

V

vacation Urlaub
vaguely ungenau
vain vergeblich
value Wert
to veer wechseln
vendor Verkäufer
vicar Pfarrer
vicarage Pfarrhaus
voice Stimme
vulnerable verletzlich

W

to wail klagen
waist Bauchumfang
to walk Gassi führen
to walk the blondes Blondinen ausführen
to walk down an aisle zum Traualtar schreiten
wallet Brieftasche
wardrobe Garderobe, Kleiderschrank
to wash up abspülen
wave Welle
to wave winken
wearily müde
weather forecast Wettervorhersage
to weep (wept – wept) weinen
to weigh something up etwas abwägen
well-briefed gut informiert
well-to-do wohlhabend
West Indies die Westindischen Inseln
to wheel ziehen

whereabouts Aufenthaltsort
to whisper flüstern
wicked verrucht
widow Witwe
widowed verwitwet
wife-swapping Partnertausch
willow gentian
Schwalbenwurzenzian
windswept windig
to wipe abwischen
wistfully wehmütig
with a spring in one's step
beschwingt
woman super Hausverwalterin
to work out ermitteln, trainieren
worn out entkräftet
worse off: to be (was/were – been)
worse off: schlecht dran sein
wretchedly elend
wrist Handgelenk
to write (wrote – written)
something off etwas abschreiben

Y

yapping kläffend
to yearn sich sehnen
youngster Kind
yucky eklig